GREAT
RESEARCH
PROJECTS
STEP BY STEP

Mary E. Mueller

J. WESTON

WALCH
PUBLISHER

Portland, Maine

Dedicated to my mother

Marjorie Jonker Hills

with love

User's Guide
to
Walch Reproducible Books

As part of our general effort to provide educational materials that are as practical and economical as possible, we have designated this publication a "reproducible book." The designation means that purchase of the book includes purchase of the right to limited reproduction of all pages on which this symbol appears:

Here is the basic Walch policy: We grant to individual purchasers of this book the right to make sufficient copies of reproducible pages for use by all students of a single teacher. This permission is limited to a single teacher and does not apply to entire schools or school systems, so institutions purchasing the book should pass the permission on to a single teacher. Copying of the book or its parts for resale is prohibited.

Any questions regarding this policy or requests to purchase further reproduction rights should be addressed to:

Permissions Editor
J. Weston Walch, Publisher
321 Valley Street • P.O. Box 658
Portland, Maine 04104-0658

1   2   3   4   5   6   7   8   9   10
ISBN 0-8251-3913-9

CONTENTS

SECTION 1: PLANNING THE RESEARCH PROJECT 1

SECTION 2: THE LIBRARY: STARTING OUT WITH PRINTED RESOURCES 43

SECTION 3: USING ELECTRONIC RESOURCES 69

ACKNOWLEDGMENTS

The author thanks the Sunrise Board of Education, its administration, and her students for the opportunity to teach library research skills. She also thanks the library staffs of Jefferson College and Missouri Baptist College for their assistance in providing access to reference materials.

The author expresses appreciation to Dr. Howard Gardner for relating the concept of the eighth intelligence through personal correspondence.

The author thanks Mr. Bill Strecker and the St. Charles City/County Library for information related to the public library. Also, the author extends appreciation to Distance Learning Resource Network (DLRN) for use of the Bloom's Taxonomy reference appearing on their web site: http://www.org/tie/dlrn/blooms.html.

The author thanks Dr. Dale Guthrie, Mr. Bill Fabian, and Ms. Anne Watts for excellent library science instruction.

Finally, the author thanks her cousin, Tom Jonker, for making available the journals of her late grandfather and uncle. Last, but not least, the author thanks her husband and children for their patience and support as she pursued this project.

ABOUT THE AUTHOR

Mary Elizabeth Mueller is employed as a K–8 librarian/reading teacher in the St. Louis, Missouri, area. An educator for over 25 years, she has taught English and reading at many levels, including college composition. She has also served as a part-time reference librarian in the St. Charles City/County Library District.

Ms. Mueller holds a B.S.S.E. in English and social studies (John Brown University), an M.S.E. in reading education (University of Central Arkansas), and an M.A. in Library Science (University of Missouri).

To the Teacher

Planning and executing successful research are, for students, often the most difficult parts of a research project. This book is designed to present some useful and time-saving techniques for conducting research, and to demystify the often overwhelming amount of information available to student researchers today.

Most research projects are designed to expand on knowledge students have already acquired in a classroom. For example, having taught a unit on the planets, a teacher may assign short individual research projects on individual planets. It is important that research evolve from an existing knowledge base; otherwise, students are likely to feel at an utter loss for where to begin their research.

Ideally, of course, research should also reflect student interest. Successful research projects, grounded in familiar information, invite the student to explore unfamiliar aspects of things or ideas they have already studied or experienced, in school or on their own. Teachers should work closely with their students to determine appropriate and interesting research subjects and to set parameters for the research.

In addition to being clear and concise, teacher expectations should be realistic, and reflect the availability of library resources and the interests and capabilities of each student. Frustration (on the part of both teacher and student) will be minimized if the research is planned cooperatively, and if teacher expectations embrace each student's individuality and promote internalization of knowledge. Students need to know "what the teacher wants" in order to feel secure, but they also need prompting to explore individual interests. Many students find it hard to articulate or discover their individual interests and will require guidance throughout the research planning process.

If the research planning process is presented clearly in sequential steps to students, research projects will proceed more smoothly. The following steps require careful teacher planning before the research process is presented to the student.

1. **Determine the scope of the research project.** The teacher must define and set parameters for the information content of the research project. Factors to consider at this stage include: (1) the interests and capabilities of the students; (2) the availability of library resources; and (3) the time frame for project completion. A fourth factor you may want to consider is the school librarian's willingness to provide assistance in information gathering. Consult the school librarian to find out about available library resources, and list those resources for student use. The Library Assistance Request Form (page 32) may be sent as an inquiry to the school librarian.

2. **Identify background knowledge** underlying the research project. What subject matter should students have mastered before beginning the research project?

For example, students cannot be expected to research individual planets if they have not first learned about the solar and planetary systems.

The first form in the teacher-related material section links sample project topics to student background knowledge, adding possible curriculum objectives (page 3).

3. **Link student background knowledge to identifiable curriculum objectives and desired mastery levels.** Student background knowledge includes understanding subject content, organizing ideas, expressing ideas correctly, and effectively using technology. The curriculum objectives also may range from broad, subject-related objectives—such as basic understanding of planet rotation—to specific, technology-related objectives—such as the ability to access a web site.

   A planning form linking background knowledge to corresponding curriculum objectives and mastery levels is included within the teacher planning section (page 4).

4. **Determine what alternatives may exist within a modified research project.** While considering possible options, teachers should also consider student differences in learning styles, cognitive ability, and reading skills.

   The teacher section includes charts that relate Bloom's Taxonomy to students' reading comprehension, ability to assimilate information, and ability to organize and use information (pages 5–6). These charts present the progression of skills needed to achieve higher-level cognitive thinking as evidenced in the analysis, synthesis, and evaluation of information. These charts are included to help teachers design suitable research projects for students who have difficulty in reading and understanding library resources.

   Charts relating student learning styles to learning modes are also included within the student-related materials section (pages 40–41). These charts will help students select research projects that better reflect their individual interests. These charts relate primarily to alternative presentation modes, suggesting options other than the traditional research paper.

5. **Establish the criteria for evaluating the research project.** In doing this, the teacher must determine basic requirements (thesis statement, theme format, mechanics, etc.) as opposed to student options (alternative presentation modes and alternative documentation).

   Evaluative criteria should reflect selected curriculum objectives and should be clearly presented to students before they begin their projects. A sample evaluative rubric is included within this section (pages 7–8).

6. **Provide management in ordering the research project.** After guiding students in selecting research topics and developing a defined information objective and corresponding outline, the teacher must provide students with a structured plan for completing the research project by breaking the project into its various components.

7. **Establish collaboration with the school librarian.** Minimum collaboration involves requesting various materials and arranging library visits; maximum collaboration requires joint planning and team instruction. Sharing teaching responsibilities requires further communication. A sample form for requesting library visits or planning team instruction, Library Media Center/Classroom Project, is included (page 13).

Students' abilities to conduct extended research projects may vary. For this reason, a variety of short research projects, cross-referenced to worksheets used in longer research projects, are included. **Exploratory research** introduces students to specific library materials in an attempt to answer specific questions. **Expository research** builds upon information found within expository text. **Literary research** analyzes authors, works, characters, and plots. **Descriptive research**, relating to the book report, provides the broad background knowledge that underlies the plot or depicts the author.

Regardless of the type of research, teacher guidance is necessary. For shorter projects, students can receive direct assistance from the teacher or librarian in organizing an information search. In longer projects, a sample checklist linking the organizational steps needed to complete the research project with corresponding due dates can help students stay on track. In both long and short projects, a student presentation project plan and student contract can be included to help the student.

Finally, a checklist for student worksheet scores is included within the teacher-related materials as a means of record keeping (page 14).

HOW TO USE THIS BOOK

The first section is directed to both teachers and students who are planning a research project. Teachers facilitating student research must provide background knowledge, concise evaluative criteria, and a management system flexible enough to encourage student exploration. Students, on the other hand, are responsible for selecting a topic within an assigned knowledge base, narrowing the topic, devising a preliminary outline, choosing a presentation mode, and collecting and documenting pertinent information. The labeled forms contained within Chapter One are arranged in teacher- and student-related material sections. The Library Assistance Request Form can be used by both teacher and student.

The second and third sections are designed to be taught in a library setting in collaboration with the school librarian. These chapters require introduction of specific print and electronic resources found in many secondary school libraries.

The fourth and fifth sections should be taught in a computer lab with Internet access. The labeled pages within these chapters introduce the student to the Internet, web sites, various search engines, and searching techniques. Collaboration with the school librarian is highly recommended.

The final section outlines general topics found on the Internet. These multi-disciplinary ideas offer students additional suggestions for research projects. The computer lab offers the best setting for investigating web sites.

TO THE STUDENT

A good research project is best completed by following a series of steps:

1. Select and narrow your research topic.

2. Determine the main idea and the best outline format for your research topic.

3. Construct a preliminary outline and complete a Research Project Planning Sheet.

4. Begin your library research. Your success in retrieving information will depend upon your ability to use the electronic card catalog and to construct search queries using keywords and Boolean operators.

5. For more current information, investigate electronic resources. On-line databases, CD-ROM databases, and the Internet are available in many homes, schools, and public and university libraries. A community network may provide you with local information.

6. Consult primary information sources. Personal e-mail, telephone conversations or personal interviews, group exchanges, diaries or journals, and artifacts are all potential sources.

7. Organize and record your information. This will be your most difficult job. While you are collecting information, you should keep track of the sources you have found. Next, you should record the information you plan to use so that you can include your data within your outline. Finally, you should record bibliographical data so that you will be able to construct a bibliography.

8. When you have finished recording and documenting your information, you should determine how to present your research project. You should also plan to complete your research project systematically and accurately. A checklist, a time planner, and a final checklist will assist you in completing your project.

SECTION 1

Planning the Research Project

Teacher Guide Page

Preplanning

The beginning of Section 1 introduces planning procedures that will help you and your students design their research projects successfully. First, assess your students' background knowledge of their research topics to determine if they will understand what they are researching. If they do, use the approach shown on page 3, Linking Background Knowledge to the Research Project, to develop project objectives that extend their background knowledge. Next, use the form on page 4, Linking Background Knowledge to Research Project Objectives and Mastery Levels, to define desired mastery levels within the project components: the depth of the subject to be researched, student technology proficiency, student research skills, and student organizational and recording skills. Then, use the charts on pages 5 and 6, Bloom's Taxonomy as Applied to the Research Project and Reading and Information Literacy Skills, to determine whether your students' reading and information literacy levels fit the type of project you wish to assign. Finally, use the Evaluative Rubric (pages 7–8), Major Mechanical Errors (page 9), and the Student Contract (page 10) as a means of evaluating each research project.

Planning the Research Project

The next part of Section 1 will help you guide your students through research planning. Use Worksheet 1A, Research Process Steps and Date Due Checklist (page 11), and Worksheet 1B, Presentation Project Plan (page 12), in developing an overall plan for a research project. Use the Library Media Center/Classroom Project Form (page 13) to schedule library visits. If your students need to become more familiar with library resources, have them use the Student Worksheet Checklist (page 14)

as they complete the library resource exercises found in subsequent chapters.

Steps in the Research Project

The final part of Section 1 will help you guide students through individual steps in their research projects. Use Selecting and Narrowing the Topic (page 15) to help students focus in on manageable, valid research topics. Use Worksheet 1C, Defining the Information Objective (page 16), to aid students in further developing their topics.

Use Worksheets 1D-1 to 1D-4, Defining the Information Objective in Exploratory Research, Defining the Information Objective in Expository Research, Defining the Information Objective in Literary Research, and Finding the Descriptive Information Objective: Researching the Book Report (pages 17–20) for planning shorter research projects that require no thesis. These projects, targeted to a more specific objective, tend to be more fact-finding in nature and are recommended for younger students. Use optional worksheets, listed at the bottom of each Worksheet 1D page, as needed.

Longer Research Projects

Longer research projects will require additional student instruction and teacher supervision. Use Developing a Variant Information Objective: The Thesis Statement (page 21) and Sample Thesis Statement/Theme Body Diagram (page 22) to help students construct their thesis statements. Use Worksheet 1E, Framing the Information Objective (pages 23–25), and the Combination Pattern Outline (page 26), Sample Combination Outline (page 27), and Outline Form(Worksheet 1F) (page 28) to help students select the outlining styles most suitable for their topics. The handouts Research Project Planning Sheet (Worksheet 1G) (page 29), The Information Pyramid (page 30), Organizing the Information Search (Worksheet 1H) (page 31), Planning Your Library Visit (page 32), and Collecting Information (page 33) will facilitate pre-research planning. The diagram in The Information Pyramid can be used to introduce various information sources to students. The handouts Recording Your Findings (page 34), Recording Source Material (page 35), and Documenting Your Research (page 36) will help students record and document their work and their findings using proper techniques and editorial style. Finally, use Worksheet 1I, Checklist for Completing the Research Process (page 37), Worksheet 1J, Time Planner for Completing the Research Process (page 38), and the Checklist for Finishing the Research Project

(page 39) as methods of keeping your students on task.

Presenting the Research Project

It can be enjoyable to help your students present their research projects. Use the student survey (Worksheet 1K), Dominant Learning Style Survey (page 40), to give students insight into their learning styles before they undertake their project designs. Use the chart in Selecting a Presentation Mode (page 41) to encourage students to choose a mode that best reflects their personality and interests.

And finally, relax, and enjoy teaching your students how to research their very best projects!

LINKING BACKGROUND KNOWLEDGE TO THE RESEARCH PROJECT

Project Topic	Necessary Background Knowledge	Possible Research Project Objectives
American National Parks	Understanding of the concept of a national park Knowledge of plant/animal wildlife Knowledge of United States geography	The student will list plants and animals existing in one national park.
American Poets	Understanding of the genre of poetry Recognition of famous American poets	The student will link each of five famous American poets to a masterpiece poem.
American Presidents	Ability to relate an American president to an era within American history	The student will relate American presidents to specific events.
Classic and Antique Cars	Knowledge of American transportation in the 1880–1920 era Knowledge of early American cars and their inventors Knowledge of the characteristics of early cars	The student will be able to describe the characteristics of early American cars and name early models.
Endangered Species	Knowledge of causes responsible for creating endangered animals and laws protecting endangered species Identification of endangered animals and their natural habitats	The student will be able to identify several endangered animals and their natural habitats.

LINKING BACKGROUND KNOWLEDGE TO RESEARCH PROJECT OBJECTIVES AND MASTERY LEVELS

Project Background Knowledge	Research Project Objectives	Project Mastery Levels
Subject Content:		
Organization:		
Mechanics:		
Technology:		

Teacher Guide Page

BLOOM'S TAXONOMY AS APPLIED TO THE RESEARCH PROJECT

HIGHER-LEVEL THINKING SKILLS	Evaluating Information **Level 6 — Evaluation** appraise, argue, assess, attach, choose, compare, defend, estimate, evaluate, judge, predict, rate, select, support, value
ABILITY TO ORGANIZE AND USE INFORMATION	Reorganizing Information **Level 5 — Synthesis** arrange, assemble, collect, compose, construct, create, design, develop, formulate, manage, organize, plan, prepare, propose, set up, write
	Analyzing Information **Level 4 — Analysis** analyze, appraise, calculate, categorize, compare, contrast, criticize, differentiate, discriminate, distinguish, examine, experiment, question, test
ABILITY TO ASSIMILATE INFORMATION	Applying Information **Level 3 — Application** apply, choose, demonstrate, dramatize, employ, illustrate, interpret, operate, practice, schedule, sketch, solve, use, write
	Understanding Information **Level 2 — Comprehension** classify, describe, discuss, explain, express, identify, indicate, locate, recognize, report, restate, review, select, translate
READING MASTERY	Remembering Information **Level 1 — Knowledge** arrange, define, duplicate, label, list, memorize, name, order, recognize, relate, recall, repeat, reproduce, state

READING AND INFORMATION LITERACY SKILLS

Level	Skill
1: Knowledge	• Library materials must match reading comprehension level of student, or, preferably, be one level below student's reading comprehension level. • Students must be able to skim and scan library materials. • Students must be familiar with arrangement of library resources commonly used in research and know how to use these resources. • Students must understand purpose for research.
2: Comprehension	• Students must possess Level 1 skills. • Students must develop defined research questions. • Students must understand the concept of keywords and be able to ascertain keywords pertaining to their questions. • Students must be familiar with search strategies. • Students must be able to determine which library resource is the most appropriate when answering a given question.
3: Application	• Students must possess Level 1 and 2 skills. • Students must be able to interpret library materials. • Students must be able to answer defined, interpretative questions. • Students must be able to devise a strategy for transferring information. • Students must be able to transfer information from a specific source. • Students must be able to reorganize information according to a specific format.
4: Analysis	• Students must possess Level 1, 2, and 3 skills. • Students must be able to devise a strategy for appraising, differentiating, and categorizing information. • Students must be able to transfer categorized information from a specific source or sources. • Students must be able to reorganize categorized information according to a specific format.
5: Synthesis	• Students must possess Level 1, 2, 3, and 4 skills. • Students must be able to recognize information, which can be arranged and utilized to support an original idea. • Students must be able to devise a strategy for collecting information from source material to a schema supporting an original idea. • Students must be able to reorganize information to support an original idea.
6: Evaluation	• Students must possess Level 1, 2, 3, 4, and 5 skills. • Students must be able to assess and judge the validity of information within its context and for its stated purpose. • Students must be able to ascertain the value of information, using standards.

From *Taxonomy of Educational Objectives* by Benjamin S. Bloom. Copyright © 1956 by Longman. Copyright renewed 1984 by Benjamin S. Bloom and David R. Krathwohl. Reprinted by permission of Addison Wesley Educational Publishers Inc.

EVALUATIVE RUBRIC

Topic Selection (10 pts.)
1. Appropriateness (5 pts.)
2. Manageability (5 pts.)

The Information Objective/Outline (15 pts.)
1. Main Idea/Position (5 pts.)
   (a) Stated clearly (3 pts.)
   (b) Backed by points/supports reflecting equal value (1 pt.)
   (c) Backed by points/supports reflecting the same meaning relationship (causes, results) (1 pt.)
2. Points/Supports (5 pts.)
   (a) Stated clearly (2 pts.)
   (b) Parallel structure (1 pt.)
   (c) Listed in appropriate order (2 pts.)
3. Outline (5 pts.)
   (a) Reflects information objective (3 pts.)
   (b) Lists specific examples in correct order (1 pt.)
   (c) Correct outline format (1 pt.)

The Project (20 pts.)
1. Main idea reflected clearly throughout project (5 pts.)
2. Theme body corresponds to points/supports (5 pts.)
   (a) Points/supports are discussed in order (1 pt.)
   (b) Points/supports introduce at least one paragraph, which further cites specific examples (4 pts.)
3. Points/supports are grounded by relevant, specific examples (5 pts.)
4. Points/supports are discussed evenly (3 pts.)
5. Information cited is complete (2 pts.)

Mechanics (10 pts.) One point is deducted for each error type:
1. Sentence fragment
2. Comma splice
3. Fused sentence
4. Lack of agreement of subject/verb
5. Wrong verb form
6. Lack of agreement of clear pronoun reference
7. Wrong pronoun case
8. Dangling modifier
9. A phrase or subordinate clause set off with a semicolon

(continued)

EVALUATIVE
RUBRIC *(continued)*

10. Wrong plural form
11. Misspelling or confusion in use of simple words
12. _____ misspelled words
13. Any garbled or incoherent sentence of any kind

The Research Process (20 pts.)

1. Current or relevant information (10 pts.)
2. Variety of information sources (5 pts.)
   (a) Print
   (b) Electronic
3. Complete information (5 pts.)

Documentation (10 pts.)

1. Recorded bibliographical information on index cards or alternative documentation (5 pts.)
   (a) Charts
   (b) Computer presentation programs
   (c) Web sites
   (d) Posters
   (e) Collages
   (f) Typed recordings
   (g) Other
2. Bibliographical information recorded according to MLA documentation style (5 pts.)
   (a) Bibliography (Works Cited) is correctly formatted (3 pts.).
   (b) All sources are listed (2 pts.).

Presentation Mode (10 pts.)

1. Concise, timely presentation (5 pts.)
2. Originality (3 pts.)
3. Delivery (poise/eye contact) (2 pts.)

Final grade: _____

Teacher comments: _____

_____

_____

_____

_____

_____

MAJOR MECHANICAL ERRORS

1. **Sentence Fragment:** Because I was tired.

2. **Comma Splice:** I like her, she is my friend.

3. **Fused Sentence:** I like her she is my friend.

4. **Lack of Subject/Verb Agreement:** He don't like spinach.

5. **Wrong Verb Form:** He lay his book down.

6. **Lack of Agreement of Clear Pronoun Reference:** Each person should do their share.

7. **Wrong Pronoun Case:** Mom told we girls to wash the dog.

8. **Dangling Modifier:** When only nine, we took him on a trip.

9. **A Phrase or Subordinate Clause Set Off with a Semicolon:**
   After going to the store; we drove home.

10. **Wrong Plural Form:** The freshman were at the game.

11. **Misspelling or Confusion in the Use of Simple Words:** I was to tired to drive home.

12. **Any Three Misspelled Words**

13. **Garbled or Incoherent Sentences:** Did it ever occur to you the money you spend?

STUDENT CONTRACT

Name _____

Class _____

RESEARCH PROJECT GRADING CRITERIA

"A" Project

Topic narrowed concisely
Body clearly corresponding to the main idea/thesis statement
Excellent information establishing main idea/thesis statement
Excellent information establishing points/supports
Research process reflected by relevant information, including original sources
Correct citations/complete bibliographical information
Desired page length
_____ major mechanical errors
Superior/original presentation mode
Handed in on time

"B" Project

Topic narrowed satisfactorily
Body corresponding to the main idea/thesis statement
Good information establishing main idea/thesis statement
Good information establishing points/supports
Research process reflected by relevant information
Correct citations/complete bibliographical information
Desired page length
_____ major mechanical errors
Excellent presentation mode
Handed in on time

"C" Project

Topic narrowed adequately
Body relating to the main idea/thesis statement
Adequate information establishing main idea/thesis statement
Adequate information establishing points/supports
Research process reflected by adequate information
Correct citations/complete bibliographical information
Desired page length
_____ major mechanical errors
Satisfactory presentation mode
Handed in on time

■ ■

Contracted grade: _____

Student signature: _____

Name _____   Date _____

RESEARCH PROCESS STEPS AND DATE DUE CHECKLIST

Research Process Steps	Date Due
Topic Selection	
Main Idea/Thesis Statement	
Preliminary Outline	
Research Project Planning Sheet	
Source Materials (index cards)	
Documentation (index cards)	
Bibliography	
Presentation Project Plan	
Final Project	
Project Presentation	

Name _____ Date _____

PRESENTATION PROJECT PLAN

1. Presentation mode _____

2. How will project be presented? _____

   _____

   _____

3. Presentation will include the following items:

   Main Idea/Thesis Statement _____

   Preliminary Outline _____

   Research Project Planning Sheet _____

   Source Materials (index cards) _____

   Documentation (index cards) _____

   Bibliography _____

4. Art forms/music forms/realia (artifacts) to be included: _____

   _____

   _____

5. Special equipment needed: _____

   _____

6. Guests: _____

   _____

7. Time needed for project presentation: _____

■■■

   Teacher comments: _____

   _____

   _____

   _____

   _____

   _____

LIBRARY MEDIA CENTER/ CLASSROOM PROJECT FORM

Teacher: _____

Class: _____

Date of Plan: _____

Date of Library Visit: _____

Objectives: _____

_____

_____

Resources Needed: _____

_____

_____

Special Instructions: _____

_____

_____

Tasks:

    Teacher: _____

    _____

    _____

    Librarian: _____

    _____

    _____

Evaluation:

_____

_____

_____

_____

STUDENT WORKSHEET CHECKLIST

Student Name _____

Project Topic _____

Worksheet No.	Points Earned	Total Points	Worksheet No.	Points Earned	Total Points
1A			3A		8
1B			3B		7
1C			3C		18
1D			3D		17
1E			3E		12
1F			4A		10
1G			4B		8
1H			4C		11
1I			4D		14
1J			4E		14
1K			4F		8
2A		20	4G		9
2B		15	4H		5
2C		19	5A		16
2D		20	5B		
2E		10	5C		
2F		15			
2G		13			
2H		13			
2I		15			
2J		11			
2K		20			

Total Points Possible: _____

Student Total Points: _____

SELECTING AND NARROWING THE TOPIC

Broad Topic (how, when, where, why?)
Narrowed Topic (subtopic or new topic)
Main Idea
Supportive Points
Examples

Criteria for Narrowing Topics

1. Think of an interesting aspect of your topic. (Hint: how, when, where, why did your topic occur?)

2. Try to limit your topic or think of a subtopic as a new topic:
   (a) Do not select a subtopic that is so broad it cannot be broken into three or four supportive points (e.g., the topic of animals).
   (b) Do not select a subtopic that is so narrow it cannot be broken into supportive points or cannot generate supporting examples (e.g., the effect of rain on baseball games in Iowa).
   (c) Do select a topic that is broad enough to allow for three or four supportive points that can be established by specific examples. For example, the topic of mountain-climbing dangers could be supported by incidents on Mt. Everest, Mt. Whitney, and Mt. Rainier.

Other Considerations in Narrowing Topics

1. The length of the paper in respect to the topic: Can the supportive points and examples within the topic be adequately discussed?

2. The type and availability of library resources: Will library resources be accessible?

3. The time frame allotted to finishing the research assignment: Will there be enough time to complete research?

Name _____ Date _____

DEFINING THE
INFORMATION OBJECTIVE

> An information objective is formulated from a narrowed topic that has a defined purpose or main idea. An information objective provides a research plan for gathering supportive examples.

Broad Topic: _____

Narrowed Topic: _____

Main Idea: _____

Supportive Points: _____

_____

_____

Examples: _____

_____

_____

Outline Pattern: _____

Preliminary Outline: _____

Presentation Mode: _____

■■

Teacher comments: _____

_____

_____

_____

_____

Name _____ Date _____

DEFINING THE INFORMATION OBJECTIVE IN EXPLORATORY RESEARCH

> An information objective formulated from a narrowed question becomes the basis for exploratory research.

Topic: _____

Narrowed Topic: _____

Research Question: _____

Sources:

    Print:

        1. _____

        2. _____

    Electronic:

        1. _____

        2. _____

        3. _____

Answer: _____

_____

Presentation Mode: _____

Additional Worksheets:

___ Presentation Project Plan (1B)

___ Framing the Information Objective: General-to-Specific (1E)

___ Organizing the Information Search (1H)

___ Collecting Information

___ Documentation

___ Dominant Learning Style Survey

___ Designing the Research Project

___ Selecting a Presentation Mode

___ Alternate Presentation Modes

___ Checklist for Completing the Research Process (1I)

Name _____   Date _____

DEFINING THE INFORMATION OBJECTIVE IN EXPOSITORY RESEARCH

An information objective in expository research is the main point supported by general details or facts. Expository research gathers these facts.

Main Idea: _____

Research Question: _____

Supportive Details/Facts: Sources:

  1. _____

  2. _____

  3. _____

  4. _____

  5. _____

Presentation Mode: _____

■■■

Teacher comments: _____

_____

_____

_____

_____

Additional worksheets:

___ Presentation Project Plan (1B)
___ Framing the Information Objective: (1E)
   ___ General-to-Specific
   ___ Sequence/Process
   ___ Cause/Effect
___ Outline Form (1F)
___ Research Project Planning Sheet (1G)
___ Organizing the Information Search (1H)
___ Collecting Information
___ Recording Your Findings

___ Recording Source Material
___ Documenting Your Research
___ Dominant Learning Style Survey
___ Designing the Research Project
___ Selecting a Presentation Mode
___ Alternate Presentation Modes
___ Checklist for Completing the Research Process (1I)
___ Time Planner for Completing the Research Process (1J)
___ Checklist for Finishing the Research Project

Name _____ Date _____

DEFINING THE INFORMATION OBJECTIVE IN LITERARY RESEARCH

An information objective originates from critical analysis of an author, a literary work, its plot, character, or set of characters. An information objective reflects a specific question concerning these literary elements.

Literary Work: _____

Research Question: _____

Information Objective: _____

Sources:

   Print:

      1. _____

      2. _____

      3. _____

   Electronic:

      1. _____

      2. _____

      3. _____

Suggested Outlines:

General-to-Specific   Problem/Solution   Cause/Effect   Comparison/Contrast

■■

Teacher comments: _____

_____

_____

_____

Additional Worksheets:

___ Presentation Project Plan (1B)

___ Outline Form (1F)

___ Research Project Planning Sheet (1G)

___ Organizing the Information Search (1H)

___ Collecting Information

___ Recording Your Findings

___ Recording Source Material

___ Documenting Your Research

___ Dominant Learning Style Survey

___ Designing the Research Project

___ Selecting a Presentation Mode

___ Alternate Presentation Modes

___ Checklist for Completing the Research Process (1I)

___ Time Planner for Completing the Research Process (1J)

___ Checklist for Finishing the Research Project

Name _____ Date _____

FINDING THE DESCRIPTIVE INFORMATION OBJECTIVE: RESEARCHING THE BOOK REPORT

The information objective provides background knowledge related to the author, characters, or plot.

Book Title: _____

Author: _____

Plot Summary (6–8 sentences): _____

_____

_____

_____

_____

_____

_____

_____

_____

Research Question: _____

_____

Information Objective (related to the author, characters, plot): _____

_____

Presentation Mode: _____

■ ■

Teacher comments: _____

_____

_____

_____

Suggested Outline:	Author:	General-to-Specific
	Plot:	Process/Sequence
		Problem/Solution
		Cause/Effect

Additional Worksheets:

___ Outline Form (1F)

___ Research Project Planning Sheet (1G)

___ Organizing the Information Search (1H)

___ Collecting Information

___ Recording Your Findings

___ Recording Source Material

___ Documenting Your Research

___ Dominant Learning Style Survey

___ Designing the Research Project

___ Selecting a Presentation Mode

___ Alternate Presentation Modes

___ Checklist for Completing the Research Process (1I)

DEVELOPING A VARIANT INFORMATION OBJECTIVE: THE THESIS STATEMENT

The **thesis statement** is the backbone of any research project, and provides organization for the project. It centers upon a main idea and is expounded upon in three supports.

The thesis statement is a position, opinion, or belief regarding the topic. This viewpoint is supported by three related aspects of the topic. These prongs verify the position and are in turn supported by specific examples. For example, the topic, the danger of hurricanes, could be stated within the following thesis statement:

> *The danger of hurricanes is evident in numerous injuries,*
> *widespread damage, and mounting cost.*

The thesis statement may include words such as ***because, due, since, for***, or include the **colon, (:)**, to introduce supports, as reflected within the following examples:

> *I like Christmas* (position) *because of its wonderful treats,*
> *glittering decorations, and festive gifts* (supports).
> *I enjoy the following Christmas holiday customs: wonderful*
> *treats, glittering decorations, and festive gifts.*

Finally, the supports within the thesis statement should be equal in meaning relationship (causes, effects, etc.) to the position. As supports, they should be of equal value and importance. Supports should also be parallel in structure, having uniform word patterns. They should be descriptive statements, clauses, nouns, or adjectives.

SAMPLE THESIS STATEMENT/
THEME BODY DIAGRAM

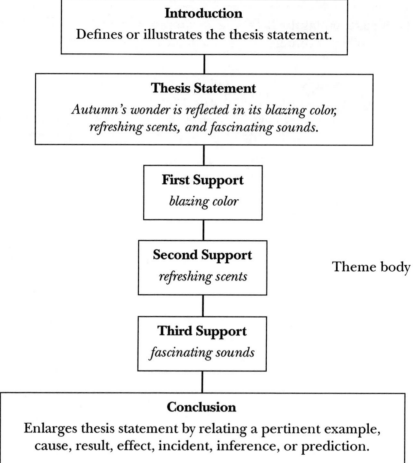

Introduction

Defines or illustrates the thesis statement.

Thesis Statement

Autumn's wonder is reflected in its blazing color, refreshing scents, and fascinating sounds.

First Support

blazing color

Second Support

refreshing scents

Theme body

Third Support

fascinating sounds

Conclusion

Enlarges thesis statement by relating a pertinent example, cause, result, effect, incident, inference, or prediction.

LINKS BETWEEN THESIS STATEMENT/THEME BODY

1. Position (autumn's wonder) and supports (blazing color, refreshing scents, and fascinating sounds) are related and have similar meanings.

2. Parallel structure of supports (all supports are descriptive adjectives ending in "ing" and specific nouns).

3. Linking words between paragraphs and subsections. The supports above can be linked through transitional words: "first," "second," and "finally."

Name _____ Date _____

FRAMING THE
INFORMATION OBJECTIVE

Outlines are efficient structures for organizing research. Some common outline patterns are diagrammed below to support various information objectives.

GENERAL-TO-SPECIFIC

_____

Title reflects the main idea or position, which will be backed by examples that follow.

I. _____
    First point/support (evidence, proof,
    example, description, or characteristic
    of the main idea)

   A. _____
       First example

   B. _____
       Second example

II. _____
    Second point/support (further
    evidence, proof, etc.)

   A. _____
       First example

   B. _____
       Second example

III. _____
    Third point/support

I. _____
    First point/support

   A. _____
       First characteristic

   B. _____
       Second characteristic

II. _____
    Second point/support

   A. _____
       First characteristic

   B. _____
       Second characteristic

III. _____
    Third point/support

Linking words between paragraphs and subsections: *actually, as a matter of fact, indeed, in fact, evidence, proof, example, specifically, for example, for instance, illustration, briefly,* etc.

SEQUENCE/PROCESS

_____

Title reflects the main idea or position of the process, which will be illustrated
by the sequence steps that follow.

I. _____
    First point/support (a step, direction, stage in the process, type, or kind)

   A. _____
       First substep

   B. _____
       Second substep

(continued)

FRAMING THE
INFORMATION OBJECTIVE *(continued)*

II. _____
    Second point/support (another step, direction, etc.)

   A. _____
    First substep

   B. _____
    Second substep

III. _____
    Third point/support

Linking words between paragraphs and subsections: *first, second, third, next, then, also, finally,* etc.

PROBLEM/SOLUTION

_____
Title reflects the position (problem).

I. _____
    First point/support (solution)

   A. _____
    First stage

   B. _____
    Second stage

II. _____
    Second point/support (solution)

   A. _____
    First step

   B. _____
    Second step

III. _____
    Third point/support (solution)

Linking words between paragraphs and subsections: *problem, a solution for, another possible solution, solved, resolved,* etc.

CAUSE/EFFECT

_____
Title reflects the position as evidenced by the points/supports; it is the point
established by the cause/effect relationship outlined below.

(continued)

FRAMING THE
INFORMATION OBJECTIVE *(continued)*

I. _____
   First point/support (a cause, reason, effect, or result)

   A. _____
        primary cause/effect

   B. _____
        secondary cause/effect

II. _____
   Second point/support (a second cause, reason, etc.)

   A. _____
        primary cause/effect

   B. _____
        secondary cause/effect

III. _____
   Third point/support

Linking words between paragraphs and subsections: *cause, explanation, motive, reason, effect, result, accordingly, as a result, consequently, for that reason, hence, then, therefore, thus,* etc.

COMPARISON/CONTRAST

_____
Title reflects the position as evidenced by the points/supports
(the comparison of like or unlike objects)

I. _____
   First point/support (an element of comparison/contrast, an alternative)

   A. _____
        First item

   B. _____
        Second item

II. _____
   Second point/support (a second element of comparison/contrast, etc.)

   A. _____
        First item

   B. _____
        Second item

III. _____
   Third point/support (element of comparison/contrast)

Linking words between paragraphs and subsections: *however, in contrast, nevertheless, on the contrary, on the other hand,* etc.

COMBINATION PATTERN OUTLINE

Dominant Pattern	Secondary Pattern
General-to-Specific	Cause/Effect Comparison/Contrast Problem/Solution Sequence/Process
Sequence/Process	General-to-Specific Problem/Solution Cause/Effect
Problem/Solution	General-to-Specific Cause/Effect Comparison/Contrast
Cause/Effect	General-to-Specific Problem/Solution Sequence/Process
Comparison/Contrast or Comparison/Alternative	Problem/Solution General-to-Specific Sequence/Process Cause/Effect

SAMPLE
COMBINATION OUTLINE

(COMBINING GENERAL-TO-SPECIFIC AND SEQUENCE/PROCESS PATTERNS)

Shopping for Prom Night

I. Clothes
   A. Determine price range
   B. Choose style and color
   C. Decide what article(s) to purchase/rent

II. Shoes
   A. Determine price range
   B. Choose style and color
   C. Decide what pair to purchase

III. Accessories
   A. Determine price range
   B. Choose style and color
   C. Decide what article(s) to purchase

Note:	The title reflects the general idea (position) backed by specific examples listed by the Roman numerals. The process pattern can be seen in the steps listed.

Name _____   Date _____

OUTLINE FORM

_____
Title

I. _____

   A. _____

      1. _____

      2. _____

   B. _____

      1. _____

      2. _____

   C. _____

      1. _____

      2. _____

II. _____

   A. _____

      1. _____

      2. _____

   B. _____

      1. _____

      2. _____

III. _____

   A. _____

      1. _____

      2. _____

   B. _____

      1. _____

      2. _____

Name _____ Date _____

RESEARCH PROJECT PLANNING SHEET

Main Idea _____

Research Strategy:

1. First Point/Support: _____

   Background Information Needed: _____

   Specialized Information Needed: _____

   Keywords: _____

   Boolean Statements: _____

2. Second Point/Support: _____

   Background Information Needed: _____

   Specialized Information Needed: _____

   Keywords: _____

   Boolean Statements: _____

3. Third Point/Support: _____

   Background Information Needed: _____

   Specialized Information Needed: _____

   Keywords: _____

   Boolean Statements: _____

Hint:	Remember to use descriptive adjectives and specific nouns as search terms. In Boolean searches, use the **AND** operator **first**. If you cannot find enough information, use the **OR** operator.

■ ■

Teacher comments: _____

_____

_____

_____

_____

_____

_____

THE INFORMATION PYRAMID

E-mail, Listservs
Chat Groups, Newsgroups
Interviews
Diaries/Journals
Art/Music forms
Realia

Level Five — Primary Sources

Web Sites
Community Networks

Level Four — The Internet

On-line, Web-based Databases
CD-ROM Databases

Level Three — Electronic Resources

Almanacs
Yearbooks
Atlases
Indexes
Consumer Guides
Government Publications

Level Two — Printed Reference Materials

Dictionaries
Encyclopedias
Books

Level One — Background Sources

Specific
to
General

Original
to
Documented

Name _____ Date _____

ORGANIZING THE INFORMATION SEARCH

Outline	Suggested Information Resources
Title _____	
I. _____	_____
A. _____	_____
1. _____	_____
2. _____	_____
B. _____	_____
1. _____	_____
2. _____	_____
II. _____	_____
A. _____	_____
1. _____	_____
2. _____	_____
B. _____	_____
1. _____	_____
2. _____	_____
C. _____	_____
1. _____	_____
2. _____	_____

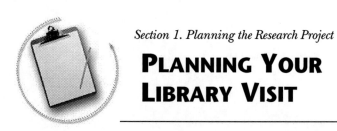

PLANNING YOUR LIBRARY VISIT

LIBRARY ASSISTANCE REQUEST FORM

Teacher/Student _____

Date _____

Nature of Request _____

_____

_____

_____

_____

_____

Date Needed _____

LIBRARY ASSISTANCE REQUEST FORM

Teacher/Student _____

Date _____

Nature of Request _____

_____

_____

_____

_____

_____

Date Needed _____

COLLECTING
INFORMATION

Level	Information Sources	Notes
1	Dictionaries Encyclopedias Books	
2	Almanacs Yearbooks Atlases Indexes Consumer guides Government publications	
3	On-line, web-based databases CD-ROM databases	
4	The Internet (web sites) Community networks	
5	E-mail, listservs Chat groups, newsgroups Interviews Diaries/journals Art/music forms Realia	

RECORDING YOUR FINDINGS

A. Use Index Cards to Record and Organize Specific Information.

Sample Outline	Sample Index Card

DEADLY TORNADOES
 	
I. First Point/Support
    A. _____
    B. _____
 	
II. Second Point/Support
    A. _____
    B. _____
	Front
	Record specific information:
	
	First Point/Support—Card 1
	pp. 100–105
	A. _____
	_____
	_____
	
	Back
	Record bibliographical information:
	
	Doe, John. *Deadly Tornadoes*. Tornado Alley: Storm Publishers, 1998.

B. Use Outline Headings to Identify and Organize Photocopied or Printed Information.

II. Second Point/Support   B.

    (highlight or underline pertinent information)

RECORDING SOURCE MATERIAL

Follow your outline in recording information:

I.	Card 1

A.
(pgs.   )

_____

_____

_____

_____

_____

I.	Card 1

B.
(pgs.   )

_____

_____

_____

_____

_____

I.	Card 1

C.
(pgs.   )

_____

_____

_____

_____

_____

Record bibliographical information on the back of your index card.

DOCUMENTING YOUR RESEARCH

Use the following citations as examples when documenting your sources. All examples follow the citation format of the Modern Language Association (MLA).

BOOK	Paulsen, Gary. *The River.* New York: Delacorte Press, 1991. author. *book title.* place of publication: publisher, date.
GENERAL ENCYCLOPEDIA	Truman, Joan. "Thanksgiving Day." *World Book Encyclopedia.* 1997 ed. author. "entry." *encyclopedia.* edition. year of publication.
SPECIAL ENCYCLOPEDIA	Mangum, Bryant. "F. Scott Fitzgerald." *Critical Survey of Long Fiction, English Language Series.* Ed. Frank Magill. 8 vols. Englewood Cliffs, NJ: Salem Press, 1983. author. "entry." *special encyclopedia.* editor. volumes. place of publication: publisher, date.
WEEKLY MAGAZINE	Rockwood, Patrick. "Science and Social Issues." *Newsweek* 5 Oct. 1987: 10–12. author. "article title." *magazine title* date: pages.
MONTHLY MAGAZINE	Poole, Ray. "The Disappearing Tiger." *National Geographic* Aug. 1998: 55–82. author. "article title." *magazine title* date: pages.
NEWSPAPER	Jones, Marianne. "Technology in the Next Century." *New York Times* 4 June 1998: A8. author. "article title." *newspaper* date: section page.
ON-LINE, WEB-BASED DATABASE magazine articles	Ans, Mae. "Your Health." *Healthy You* 4 Dec. 1998. Ebscohost. 5 Dec. 1998. <http://ebscohost.com>. author. "article title." *magazine title* publication date. database. access date. <URL>.
CD-ROM DATABASE periodicals	Hays, Ann. "Anorexia." *Medical News* 2 Nov. 1997: 124–143. *Academic Abstracts.* CD-ROM. Ebsco. 1998. author. "article title." *magazine title* date: pages. *title of database.* medium. vendor. electronic publication date.
WEB PAGE	Jay, John. *Stars.* Welcome University. 3 Oct. 1998. <http://www.welcome.edu/stars>. author. *title.* institution/organization. access date. <URL>.
E-MAIL	Beldon, David. "Hi, Mom." E-mail to Mary Mueller. 30 May 1998. sender. "subject of message." E-mail to sender. date message sent.
LISTSERV	Voulon, Ray. "Conservation Information." On-line posting. 30 May 1998. Conservation Forum. 3 July 1998. <http://www.CONSERVE@cf.com>. author. "title." medium. date. forum. access date. <URL>.
USENET	Smith, Jane. "Cosmetic Magic." On-line posting. 29 Dec. 1998. 1 Jan. 1999 <news:talk.beauty.cosmetics>. author. title. medium. posting date. access date <newsgroup>.
INTERVIEW	Doe, Jane. Personal interview. 4 June 1998. name of person interviewed. type of interview. date.

Name _____ Date _____

CHECKLIST FOR COMPLETING THE RESEARCH PROCESS

Main Idea/Thesis Statement: _____

_____

Presentation Mode: _____

	Level/Source	Information Found	Information Needed
1	Dictionaries Encyclopedias Books		
2	Almanacs Yearbooks Atlases Indexes Consumer guides Government publications		
3	On-line databases CD-ROM databases		
4	Web sites Community network		
5	E-mail, listservs Chat/newsgroups Interviews Diaries/journals Art/music forms Realia		

Name _____ Date _____

TIME PLANNER FOR COMPLETING THE RESEARCH PROCESS

Steps within the Research Process	Date Due	Date Completed
1. Topic Selection	_____	_____
2. Main Idea/Thesis Statement	_____	_____
3. Preliminary Outline	_____	_____
First Point/Support		_____
Second Point/Support		_____
Third Point/Support		_____
4. Research Project Planning Sheet	_____	_____
5. Source Material (index cards)	_____	_____
First Point/Support		_____
Second Point/Support		_____
Third Point/Support		_____
6. Documentation (index cards)	_____	_____
First Point/Support		_____
Second Point/Support		_____
Third Point/Support		_____
7. Bibliography	_____	_____
8. Presentation Mode	_____	_____
9. Final Project	_____	_____
10. Project Presentation	_____	_____

CHECKLIST FOR FINISHING THE RESEARCH PROJECT

Project Components	Criteria Items
Main Idea/ Thesis Statement	clearly stated grounded by background research specified by concrete examples
Research Process	reflects adequate background sources variety of print/electronic resources variety of web sites includes at least one primary source
Notes/Documentation	legible, well-documented index cards organized by outline headings headings on printed sources reflect outline headings bibliographical information is recorded bibliography completed, using MLA format
Project Outline	reflects information objective well-organized pattern or pattern combination format clearly stated reflects general points as background sources and specific examples as current sources
Presentation	complements the project information reflects student's individual style promotes student's interest in research

Name _____ Date _____

DOMINANT LEARNING STYLE SURVEY

The questions below will help you determine how you learn best. Use the chart on page 41 to select a way to present your research project that is compatible with your learning style(s).

Choose one response for each question below. Then use the key at the bottom of this page to identify your dominant learning style(s).

1. I would choose to do the following activity in my free time:

    _____ (a) read a book or magazine   _____ (e) exercise/play a sport

    _____ (b) take something apart   _____ (f) talk to friends

    _____ (c) do artwork   _____ (g) work on an original project

    _____ (d) listen to the radio   _____ (h) go on a nature walk

2. In school, my first choice is for lessons that involve:

    _____ (a) reading/writing   _____ (e) physical movement

    _____ (b) problem solving   _____ (f) group interaction

    _____ (c) drawing   _____ (g) individualized learning

    _____ (d) reading music   _____ (h) outdoor activities

3. My first choice for an assignment would be to:

    _____ (a) write a report   _____ (f) participate in a discussion group

    _____ (b) conduct an experiment

    _____ (c) design an art project   _____ (g) create an individual assignment

    _____ (d) prepare a music selection

    _____ (e) act in a skit   _____ (h) gather a nature collection

---

Dominant learning styles are indicated by at least two identical letter responses to the above questions. Mixed learning styles are indicated by varied letter responses. The types of learning styles are indicated by the following letters:
A. Linguistic   B. Logical-mathematical   C. Spatial   D. Musical   E. Bodily-kinesthetic   F. Interpersonal
G. Intrapersonal   H. Naturalist

SELECTING A PRESENTATION MODE

Linguistic	Logical-Mathematical	Spatial	Musical	Bodily-Kinesthetic	Interpersonal	Intrapersonal	Naturalist
book report	analysis	art form	ballad	acting	announcement	commentary	classification
book talk	coding	artifact	instrumental music	announcement	chat group	diary	collection
brochure	crossword puzzle	display	music recording	commercial	commercial	editorial	exhibit
commentary	debate	banner	recording	dance	game	e-mail	index
computer presentation	dissection	collage		demonstration	greeting	journal	nature observation
debate	game	comic strip		dialog	interview	poem	outdoor outing
description	graph	computer presentation		dramatic monologue	mock court	project	taxonomy
editorial	index	craft		interview	mock election	research paper	weather report
e-mail	mathematical equation	digital camera production		jokes	newsgroup	sampling	
fax message	model	diorama		mimicry	panel discussion	storytelling	
greeting	problem solving	display		mock court	play	story writing	
journal	prototype	painting		newscast	polling		
lecture	puzzle	photography		pantomime	reader's theater		
magazine article	scale model	portrait		play	sampling		
newsbrief	spreadsheet	poster		role-playing	show		
outline	statistics	scale model		show	skit		
poem		sculpture		skit	television broadcast		
research paper		transparencies		standup comedy			
speech		video recording		telephone conversation			
story		web site		television broadcast			
storytelling							
summary							
time line							
work order							

SECTION 2

The Library: Starting out with Printed Resources

Introducing Library Basics

The first part of Section 2 introduces the library to students unfamiliar with the Dewey Decimal Classification (DDC) system, call numbers, the card catalog, the electronic catalog, and keyword searching. Use the handout The Dewey Decimal Classification System (page 44) to introduce Dewey Decimal numbers and corresponding subject matter. Use the page DDC Numbers (Worksheet 2A) (page 45) as an optional student exercise. To introduce further card catalog information, use the handouts Call Numbers and the Card Catalog (page 46) and The Card Set (page 47). The handout Using the Card Catalog (Worksheet 2B) (page 48) is an optional student exercise.

The handout Subject Headings and the Card Set (page 49) can serve as a transitional page to the electronic catalog. Emphasize to students that the author card is the basis for both the format and bibliographical information cited in the electronic catalog. Also, emphasize that the cross-reference terms listed at the bottom of the author card are the basis for subject-related keyword search terms used in the electronic card catalog. Use the handouts The Electronic Catalog (pages 50–51) and the Sample Electronic Catalog (page 52) to intro-

duce this concept; follow up with Worksheet 2C, Using the Electronic Catalog (page 53), and Worksheet 2D, Using Keywords (page 54), to test students' ability to use keywords.

To introduce Boolean logic and how it works, use the handout Boolean Logic Operators (page 55). This can be reinforced by the activity Using Boolean Logic (Worksheet 2E) (page 56).

Introducing Library Resources

The last part of Section 2 introduces students to library resources in the order indicated by The Information Pyramid (page 30). Use Background Sources (page 57) to introduce students to dictionaries and encyclopedias. The handout Printed Reference Materials (pages 58–61) provides students with information about almanacs, fact books, yearbooks, the atlas, indexes, consumer guides, and government publications.

Finally, use student Worksheets 2F–2K, Library Resources: Finding Information (pages 62–67), to teach your students the type of information found within each reference book. Emphasize the importance of being familiar with commonly used reference books.

THE DEWEY DECIMAL CLASSIFICATION SYSTEM

Because library materials must be readily available for use, the arrangement of materials within the school library is important. All nonfiction materials are ordered by the Dewey Decimal Classification (DDC) system. This is an ordering system in which subject matter is categorized in ten broad areas:

Area	Type of Subject Matter
000–099	data processing, computer science, encyclopedias, general collections, manuscripts
100–199	paranormal phenomena, philosophical viewpoints, psychology, logic, ethics, philosophy
200–299	religion, church and religious orders, mythology
300–399	political science, economics, law, social problems, education, customs, folklore
400–499	linguistics, languages
500–599	mathematics, astronomy, physics, chemistry, paleontology, life sciences, botany, zoology
600–699	medical sciences, engineering, agriculture, home economics, manufactures, buildings
700–799	landscaping, architecture, the arts, photography, music, sports
800–899	literature
900–999	geography, travel, biographies, history

Name _____   Date _____

DDC
NUMBERS

> This exercise will help you understand the subject arrangement of library materials. Classify the imaginary titles below by their subject.

The following titles do not have classification numbers. Using your DDC chart, assign the correct area to each title.

Example: *Math for Everyone!*   *500–599*

1. *The Sun* _____

2. *Pegasus* _____

3. *Famous Pirates of the New World* _____

4. *Candies, Cookies, Cakes!* _____

5. *Time for Poetry* _____

6. *Indian Chiefs* _____

7. *Jobs in Government Service* _____

8. *Life on Earth* _____

9. *Macramé* _____

10. *Guinness Sports Record Book* _____

11. *Famous Americans* _____

12. *Viruses and the Human Body* _____

13. *Gateway to Space* _____

14. *Fairy Tales from Sweden* _____

15. *Be a Smart Shopper* _____

16. *India* _____

17. *Garden Flowers* _____

18. *The Art of the Plains Indians* _____

19. *Inside the Mind* _____

20. *Apollo in Space* _____

CALL NUMBERS AND THE CARD CATALOG

Call Numbers

All books are arranged by **call number**, or identification, noted on the spine of the book. The call number is made up of the Dewey Decimal Classification number (DDC) assigned to the book and the first three letters of the author's last name. The call number indicates the location and shelf arrangement of the book within the library.

Fiction Call Numbers

Fiction books are not included within the DDC system. Instead, they are arranged alphabetically by the first three letters of the author's last name under the designation F or FIC. Thus, the novel *Today* by John Doe would be found under the call number FIC DOE.

Master Index or Catalog

All library materials can be located through a **master index** or catalog. Whether the catalog is print or electronic, it provides access points (author, title, and subject headings) for each item held within the library.

The card catalog is arranged like a dictionary. Card sets, containing author, title, and subject cards for every item, are filed in alphabetical order. Each card set has the same book or bibliographical information, including the call number. The difference between the individual cards is the first entry or heading appearing on the first line. The first entry for the **author card** is the author's name; the first entry for the **title card** is the book title; the first entry for the **subject card** is the subject heading assigned to the book. The author card is filed alphabetically in the card catalog according to the author's last name; the title card is filed alphabetically according to the title; and the subject card is filed alphabetically according to the subject.

THE
CARD SET

Bibliographical Information:

E
JON   Jones, Jan. ————————————— **Author**
        Title ——— The mighty cat / Jan Jones.
  Description ——— __ New York : Random, 1987. ——— **Publisher**
          unp. : ill. (Happy time books) **Copyright Date**
                                        Series

  Summary ——— The mighty cat rescues her kittens
         threatened by three dogs.
            ISBN 0-333-48840-6 ——————— **ISBN number**

            1. Cat- -Fiction. 2. Dog- -Fiction. ——— **Subject Heading**
  Subject Heading ——— I. Title. II. Series

AUTHOR CARD

E
JON   The mighty cat

     Jones, Jan.
        The mighty cat / Jan Jones.
     __ New York : Random, 1987.
        unp. : ill. (Happy time books)

        The mighty cat rescues her kittens
     threatened by three dogs.
        ISBN 0-333-48840-6

     1. Cat- -Fiction. 2. Dog- -Fiction.
     I. Title. II. Series

TITLE CARD

E
JON   CAT—FICTION

     Jones, Jan.
        The mighty cat / Jan Jones.
     __ New York : Random, 1987.
        unp. : ill. (Happy time books)

        The mighty cat rescues her kittens
     threatened by three dogs.
        ISBN 0-333-48840-6

     1. Cat- -Fiction. 2. Dog- -Fiction.
     I. Title. II. Series

SUBJECT CARD

Name _____ Date _____

USING THE CARD CATALOG

This exercise will help you understand how library materials can be accessed, manually or electronically. Imagine that you are the librarian. Which card in the card catalog would you use to answer each question below?

Decide which card within the card catalog would best answer each question below. (You don't need to answer the questions—just say where you would look for the answers.) Write **A** for author card, **T** for title card, and **S** for subject card.

_____ 1. Does the library have a book about the history of France?

_____ 2. Is there a book titled *A Pumpkin in a Pear Tree?*

_____ 3. Does the library have any books by Edmund Stone?

_____ 4. Does the library have any books about predicting storms?

_____ 5. Who is the author of *When Is Now?*

_____ 6. Besides *The Little Puppy*, does the library have any other books in the Little Pet Series by Susie Sweet?

_____ 7. Has Tom Tompson written a book about animals?

_____ 8. How many books by Louis Sachar does the library have?

_____ 9. Does the library have any books about tree rings?

_____ 10. Is *Bells, Bells, Bells* in the library collection?

_____ 11. Who is the author of *Roller Races?*

_____ 12. Does the library have any books about ecology?

_____ 13. Does the library have a copy of Lea Lenner's book about fashion?

_____ 14. Is *The Velveteen Rabbit* included within the library collection?

_____ 15. Who is the author of *Little Women?*

SUBJECT HEADINGS AND THE CARD SET

The card set is indexed by the Arabic and Roman numeral headings listed at the bottom of the author card below:

```
E
JON        Jones, Jan.
                The mighty cat / Jan Jones.
              __ New York : Random, 1987.
                unp. : ill. (Happy time books)

                The mighty cat rescues her kittens
           threatened by three dogs.
                ISBN 0-333-48840-6


           1. Cat- -Fiction.  2. Dog- -Fiction.
           I. Title.  II. Series
```

In the example above, the title and series entries are indicated by I. Title and II. Series. The subject heading or headings are indicated by Arabic numeral 1. Cat- -Fiction and 2. Dog- -Fiction.

All subject headings are standard headings chosen by the Library of Congress, and are used in most school and public libraries. Not only do subject headings help index the card catalog, they have become the major access points for ordering information within the electronic catalog.

Because most information quests begin with a researcher looking up a subject, subject headings provide an important tool in locating other resources within a broad knowledge base. Subject headings are often cross-referenced by keywords and by related subject headings, which help students obtain resources in related subject matter.

Most electronic catalogs are user-friendly. Traditional subject headings, such as "Cat—fiction," are most likely cross-referenced with familiar terms, such as "cat."

THE ELECTRONIC CATALOG

The electronic catalog is a massive index in which information is organized by author, title, and subject. Like the card catalog, certain rules for accessing information apply.

Author:	Search by last name, first name, middle name order.
Title:	Search by title, excluding articles *a, an,* and *the.*
Subject:	Search by subject headings.

Subject headings within the electronic catalog are the same headings used within the card catalog and are standard in most schools and public libraries. Subject headings are the most important access point to library materials, as most students do not come to a library knowing exactly which library materials they wish to use.

Subject headings can be easily obtained through the following procedure:

1. Begin your search by using a specific author or title pertaining to your subject matter.

2. Use the author or title access to call up a specific library resource.

3. After you have found your resource, access the full record display or bibliographical information option to find the subject headings that index your resource. You will find that the full record display resembles the subject card within the card catalog.

4. Look for the SUBJECT headings listed at the bottom of the record display.

5. Copy down these subject headings and use as keywords for future searches.

6. If you cannot find desired information, begin by accessing specific subject matter related to your topic. Retrieve subject headings from bibliographical information and continue searching, using these subject headings as clues to construct new search terms.

(continued)

THE ELECTRONIC CATALOG *(continued)*

If you do not have any authors or titles from which to launch your search, try the procedure below.

1. Enter your keyword search term, for example, "cat."

2. Look at the "hit" list for specific titles and authors.

3. If the "hit" list does not include materials on your topic, try using a synonym for your keyword.

4. If the "hit" list does not include satisfactory titles, broaden or narrow your keyword.
   Narrowed keyword—Siamese cat
   Broadened keyword—Feline

5. If you still cannot find suitable material, look at the bibliographical information of the book closest to your topic. Look for the subject headings listed. They can give you clues for more keyword searches.

6. If you still cannot find any library material, ask your librarian!

SAMPLE
ELECTRONIC CATALOG

Example of display screen you might see:

> Type the following symbols plus specific information to access the electronic catalog:
>
> AU/   (author)
> TI/   (title)
> SU/   (subject)
> BI/   bibliographical information
> E/   exit
> N/   next page

AUTHOR ACCESS

> AU/Jones, Jan
>
> 1   The mighty cat

TITLE ACCESS

> TI/mighty cat
>
> 1   E JON
> 2   E JON VCR tape
> 3   E JON Recording

SUBJECT ACCESS

> SU/Cat—Fiction*
>
> 1   E JON   The Mighty Cat
> 2   E ROW   Millie the Cat
> 3   E SAN   Bad Billie

*Most electronic catalogs replace traditional subject headings with keywords. Therefore, Cat—Fiction appears as Cat.

Name _____ Date _____

USING THE ELECTRONIC CATALOG

This exercise will help you understand how library material can be accessed electronically. Without answering the questions below, determine how to find the authors, titles, or subject matter referred to within each question.

Choose the access option that would give you the information to answer the following questions:

AU/(author)
TI/(title)
SU/(subject)

_____ 1. Are there any books by Miriam Gold besides *Fame?*

_____ 2. Is there a book titled *Housebuilding for Children?*

_____ 3. Does the library have any books about making soap?

_____ 4. Are there any books by Kenneth Stone in the library?

_____ 5. Who is the author of *Fame?*

_____ 6. What are the names of some books about Panama?

_____ 7. Who is the author of *Under the Lilacs?*

_____ 8. Does the library have a biography on Jesse Owens?

_____ 9. What are the names of some books about zoos?

_____ 10. What books about dog training are in the library?

_____ 11. Are there any books by Judy Blume in the library?

_____ 12. Who wrote *Before the Supreme Court?*

_____ 13. Does the library have any books about Stonehenge?

_____ 14. Who is the author of *Exercise, Exercise!?*

_____ 15. Did Roger Thomas write *The Ice Age?*

_____ 16. How many books did Anne Macdonald write?

_____ 17. Did Jeanne Dixon write her autobiography?

_____ 18. How many biographies does the library have on Grandma Moses?

_____ 19. How many chapters are in James Jones's *World War I?*

USING KEYWORDS

> This exercise will help you select the word or words within each question that determine where the answer may be found. Do not answer the questions!

Answer the following questions by using the subject command SU/ and by adding an appropriate keyword.

Example: What is a comet? <u>SU/comet</u>

1. Who invented the Barbie doll? _____

2. How fast does the cheetah run? _____

3. How does the barometer work? _____

4. What is a solar eclipse? _____

5. When was the telephone invented? _____

6. Who was the first to land on the Moon? _____

7. What is the speed of light? _____

8. How many planets are in our solar system? _____

9. Who invented the alphabet? _____

10. How many stars are in the universe? _____

11. What are the primary colors? _____

12. How many people live in Australia? _____

13. How many players are on a baseball team? _____

14. Where are the Himalaya Mountains? _____

15. What is the average temperature in France? _____

16. What are three fire prevention rules? _____

17. Why is electricity dangerous? _____

18. Why is the winter solstice in December? _____

19. What books have won the Newbery Medal? _____

20. How far away is the Hale-Bopp comet? _____

BOOLEAN LOGIC OPERATORS

Some electronic catalogs have an additional feature called **Boolean logic**. Upon command, Boolean logic can link subject headings and keywords. For example, if you wanted to write a report on the kings of modern France, you could type the following command, using the subject access:

SU/kings AND modern France

The electronic catalog would then begin to collect all library materials indexed under kings AND modern France and to list them under the subject access.

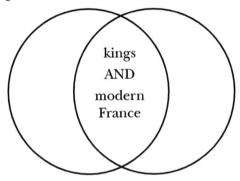

LIMITS INFORMATION SOURCES

AND

kings AND modern France

ACCESSES

All library resources indexed under "kings" and "modern France"

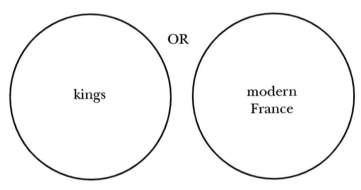

EXPANDS INFORMATION SOURCES

OR

kings OR modern France

ACCESSES

All library resources indexed under "kings" or under "modern France"

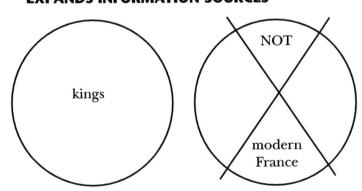

EXCLUDES INFORMATION SOURCES

NOT

kings NOT modern France

ACCESSES

All library resources indexed under "kings" but not indexed under "modern France"

Great Research Projects Step by Step

Name _____ Date _____

USING
BOOLEAN LOGIC

This exercise will help you learn how to combine terms in order to access specific information. Do not answer the questions below; instead, select keywords within each question and add Boolean operators.

The questions below can be answered by an electronic catalog, which uses Boolean operators to sort indexed keywords.

Using the subject command SU/(subject), find the answers to the questions using the Boolean operators AND, OR, and NOT between keywords.

Example	
	1. What is the difference between whales and sharks?
	SU/whales OR sharks
	2. Name the tornado with the greatest recorded wind speed.
	SU/tornado AND windspeed
	3. Name famous baseball players, excluding Babe Ruth.
	SU/baseball players NOT Babe Ruth

1. Who are the inhabitants of the Madagascar Islands?

   _____

2. What is the difference between the Arabian oryx and its relative, the scimitar-horned oryx?

   _____

3. How do the members of the whale family, excluding the blue whale, vary in size?

   _____

4. What atmosphere surrounds Jupiter? _____

5. How do crocodiles and alligators differ? _____

6. How many varieties of roses, excluding pink roses, exist?

   _____

7. What is the hottest climate zone? _____

8. What sport, excluding football, claims the most injuries?

   _____

9. What is the difference between soccer and ice hockey? _____

10. What hurricane caused the most fatalities? _____

BACKGROUND SOURCES*

Dictionaries	Content	Arrangement
Webster's Third New International Dictionary of the English Language, Unabridged	450,000+ words; parts of speech; etymology; pronunciation guide	alphabetical order
Merriam-Webster's Collegiate Dictionary	based upon 14.5 million citations; includes pronunciation guide; etymology; signs and symbols; foreign words and phrases; handbook of style	alphabetical order
Webster's New Geographical Dictionary	describes natural features, nationality, political divisions, populations; includes tables and maps	alphabetical order
Webster's New Biographical Dictionary	short biographical sketches of noteworthy persons	alphabetical order by last name
The Cambridge Thesaurus of American English	dictionary of synonyms and antonyms	alphabetical order
Bartlett's Familiar Quotations	quotations, including author and source; footnotes explaining quotations are listed chronologically by author's birthdate	indexed by author, keyword, first line
Brewer's Dictionary of Phrase and Fable	dictionary of characters, places, words, terminology, phrases, and modern slang	alphabetical order

Encyclopedias	Content	Arrangement
The World Book Encyclopedia	generalized information cross-referenced; illustrations; maps; signed entries; high readability	alphabetical order
Academic American Encyclopedia	generalized information cross-referenced; pictures; maps; signed entries; adult readability	alphabetical order
Encyclopedia Britannica	detailed information cross-referenced; pictures; charts; graphs; unsigned entries; adult readability	alphabetical order

* Some of these resources are also available on-line.

PRINTED REFERENCE MATERIALS*

Almanacs	Content	Arrangement
The World Almanac and Book of Facts	published yearly; general information	table of contents; alphabetized subject headings
Information Please Almanac: Atlas & Yearbook	published yearly; general information	table of contents; alphabetized subject headings
The World Almanac of the USA	information on United States as a whole; on the fifty states, regions, and territories; and comparison charts between the states	parts I, II, and indexed by alphabetized subject headings
The New York Public Library Desk Reference	general information	table of contents; subject headings
The New York Times Almanac	published yearly; general information	table of contents; alphabetized subject headings

Fact Books/Yearbooks	Content	Arrangement
Famous First Facts: A Record of First Happenings, Discoveries, and Inventions in American History	first occurrences	alphabetical subject headings; indexed by year, days, names; geographical index
The Guinness Book of Records	records established	alphabetically indexed by broad and specific subject headings
Masterplots II	juvenile and young adult fiction titles arranged in three subsections: (1) the story; (2) themes and meanings; and (3) context	alphabetically indexed by title
Contemporary Authors: A Bio–bibliographical Guide to Current Authors and Their Works	information about authors of poetry, fiction, and nonfiction currently published and read	alphabetical order by author's last name

* Some of these resources are also available on-line.

(continued)

PRINTED
REFERENCE MATERIALS* *(continued)*

Fact Books/Yearbooks	Content	Arrangement
Magill's Literary Annual	published yearly; evaluates outstanding works on history, biography, autobiography, diaries, letters, current affairs, social science, and science	subject headings indexed by author's last name
Current Biography Yearbook	published yearly; biographical articles about living worldwide leaders, including individuals who died during the year	alphabetical order by last name
Facts on File	published yearly; weekly news digest with cumulative index; atlas included	alphabetically indexed by subject headings
The Europa World Year Book	published yearly; lists facts related to individual countries; statistical tables	alphabetical order by country
Yearbook of the United Nations	published yearly; United Nations proceedings: political, security, regional, economic, social and legal concerns; United Nations organizations	indexed by subject headings and sub-headings

Atlas	Content	Arrangement
National Geographic Atlas of the World	physical and political world and continental maps	indexed by continents, oceans, and worlds beyond

Indexes	Content	Arrangement
*Reader's Guide to Periodical Literature***	published yearly; cites title(s) related to subject headings and gives complete bibliographical information for magazine article(s) listed	alphabetical subject headings

* Some of these resources are also available on-line.

** The print edition of *Reader's Guide to Periodical Literature* is found in most public libraries. Having been published for over 100 years, this annual index currently covers over 170 periodicals (magazines) of general interest. This popular periodical index is also available on CD-ROM and as an on-line database.

(continued)

PRINTED REFERENCE MATERIALS* *(continued)*

Indexes	Content	Arrangement
National Geographic Index	published yearly; cites title(s) related to subject headings and gives complete bibliographical information for magazine article(s) listed	alphabetical subject headings
The Columbia Granger's Index to Poetry	title, first line and last line index; author index; subject index	alphabetical order
Short Story Index	lists authors, titles, and subjects related to short stories	alphabetical author, title, and subject headings
The New York Times Index	annual index; lists articles by titles under subject headings	alphabetical subject headings

Consumer Guides	Content	Arrangement
N.A.D.A. Official Older Used Car Guide: An Official N.A.D.A. Value Guide	published three times a year; lists retail price, trade-in value, and loan value of vehicle models	alphabetical order by manufacturer and model
Edmund's: New Car Guide	published yearly; reviews model and standard equipment; lists manufacturer's suggested retail price and dealer's invoice for listed vehicles	alphabetical order by manufacturer and model
Consumer Reports Buying Guide	published yearly; describes the appliance and its features, lists appliance by model and price	subject headings categorizing appliances
Best Buys & Discount Prices	published yearly; lists appliances, describes model, states warranty, retail price, low price, and recommends model	category and sub-category list models

* Some of these resources are also available on-line.

(continued)

PRINTED
REFERENCE MATERIALS* *(continued)*

Government Publications	Content	Arrangement
Congressional Quarterly Almanac	published yearly; cites proceedings and issues related to congressional year	indexed alphabetically by subject matter
Official Congressional Directory	published yearly; cites members, officers, committees, departments, and organizations related to the legislative, executive, and judicial branches of the federal government	indexed alphabetically by subject
Statistical Abstract of the United States	published yearly, cites statistics related to the United States; tables and graphs	subject matter
Statistical Abstract of the World	published yearly, cites statistics related to individual countries; tables and graphs	alphabetical order by countries

* Some of these resources are also available on-line.

Name _____ Date _____

LIBRARY RESOURCES: FINDING INFORMATION

This exercise will help you become familiar with the type of information found in each reference book. Do not answer the questions below; instead, determine where you would find each answer.

Atlas: A map book
Almanac: An annual book of current facts
Encyclopedia: An alphabetically ordered, definitive reference book
Biographical dictionary: An alphabetically ordered reference book of famous persons
Geographical dictionary: An alphabetically ordered reference book of places in the world

Decide whether an atlas, an almanac, an encyclopedia, a biographical dictionary, or a geographical dictionary would best help you find the information requested below. Write the type of reference book next to each question.

1. What state is east of Iowa? _____

2. What is the current population of Nevada? _____

3. Who is Thomas Edison? _____

4. What are the characteristics of a Siberian tiger? _____

5. What is the main industry of the Virgin Islands? _____

6. Where are the Appalachian Mountains? _____

7. What is the capital of France? _____

8. Who was Harry S. Truman? _____

9. What teams played in last year's World Series? _____

10. What poems were written by Emily Dickinson? _____

11. Are there any towns in Antarctica? _____

12. What hurricanes have recently hit the United States? _____

13. What laws were recently passed in the United States? _____

14. What was the first computer? _____

15. List ten countries other than the United States. _____

_____

_____

LIBRARY RESOURCES: FINDING INFORMATION

This exercise will help you become familiar with the type of information found in each reference book.

You can find information for your report by using the following reference books:

Thesaurus: Dictionary of synonyms
National Geographic Index: A topical index of *National Geographic* issues
Reader's Guide to Periodical Literature: A topical index of magazines
Bartlett's Book of Familiar Quotations: A topically arranged book of quotations
Brewer's Dictionary of Phrase and Fable: A dictionary of literary terms, phrases, and modern slang

Decide which reference book above is the best source of information for each topic below. Write the title of that reference book next to the topic.

1. the person who said "time does not relinquish its rights" _____

2. the death of Jacqueline Onassis _____

3. white Siberian tigers _____

4. the tortoise and the hare _____

5. Mt. Everest and the Himalayas _____

6. Jupiter _____

7. "love" sayings _____

8. the Rolling Stones _____

9. synonym of "antiquity" _____

10. quotations by James Monroe _____

11. man's first visit to the Moon _____

12. 2000 election _____

13. Aesop _____

LIBRARY RESOURCES: FINDING INFORMATION

This exercise will help you become familiar with the type of information found in each reference book.

You can find information for your report by using the following reference books:

> ***Famous First Facts:*** A book listing first occurrences in American history
> ***The Guinness Book of Records:*** A yearly issue listing records established in all categories
> ***Masterplots II:*** A synopsis and analysis of well-known juvenile and young adult fiction titles
> ***Contemporary Authors: A Bio-bibliographical Guide to Current Authors and Their Works:*** A book series discussing the life and works of current authors
> ***Magill's Literary Annual:*** A book evaluating outstanding literary works published during the current year
> ***Short Story Index:*** An index listing authors, titles, and subjects related to short stories

Decide which reference book listed above is the best source of information for each topic below. Write the title of that reference book next to the topic.

1. *The Last of the Mohicans* _____

2. the life of John Grisham _____

3. a critique on the most recent Newbery Award winner _____

4. the most coffee consumed in one sitting _____

5. the first stop sign _____

6. a commentary on *The Diary of Anne Frank* _____

7. a synopsis of *Tom Sawyer* _____

8. the plot of *The Good Earth* _____

9. *The Gift of the Magi* _____

10. the setting of *A Tale of Two Cities* _____

11. the childhood of Maya Angelou _____

12. critique on the most recent Pulitzer Prize fiction winner _____

13. O. Henry _____

Name _____ Date _____

LIBRARY RESOURCES: FINDING INFORMATION

This exercise will help you become familiar with the type of information found in each reference book.

You can find information for your report by using the correct issue of the following yearbooks:

Current Biography Yearbook: A book of biographical articles about living world leaders; obituaries
Facts on File: Weekly news updates, cumulatively indexed
The Europa World Year Book: Cites facts related to individual countries
Yearbook of the United Nations: Cites United Nations proceedings

Decide which yearbook is the best source for each of the following topics. Write the title of that yearbook next to the topic.

1. the dominant religion of South Africa _____

2. an account of the Great Flood of 1993 _____

3. the life of Tony Blair _____

4. world reaction to Iran's military growth _____

5. peacekeeping mission in Bosnia _____

6. the languages of India _____

7. Mother Teresa's funeral _____

8. Norwegian climate _____

9. United Nations committees _____

10. Princess Diana's death _____

11. Russian space missions _____

12. renovation of the Sphinx _____

13. searching for the *Titanic* remains _____

14. Dutch exports _____

15. lawsuits against tobacco companies _____

Name _____ Date _____

LIBRARY RESOURCES:
FINDING INFORMATION

This exercise will help you become familiar with the type of information found in each reference book.

You can find information for your report by using the following reference books:

N.A.D.A. Official Older Used Car Guide: A book listing current retail price, trade-in value, and loan value for vehicle models
Consumer Reports Buying Guide: A book describing appliances and their features, listing model and price
Congressional Quarterly Almanac: A book that cites proceedings and issues relating to the congressional year
Official Congressional Directory: A book listing members, committees, departments, and organizations related to the executive, legislative, and judicial government branches
Statistical Abstract of the United States: A book citing statistics related to the United States
Statistical Abstract of the World: A book citing statistics related to all countries

Decide which reference book is the best source of information for each of the following topics. Write the title of that reference book next to the topic.

1. the senators representing North Dakota _____

2. rainfall during 1996 in the midwestern United States _____

3. Japanese literacy rate _____

4. the average retail price of a 1996 Honda LX Accord _____

5. the most economical air conditioning unit _____

6. the cabinet members of the United States government _____

7. the lowest crime area within the United States _____

8. the Supreme Court justices _____

9. Internal Revenue hearings _____

10. comparison of the price of garbage disposals _____

11. international value of the American dollar _____

Name _____ Date _____

LIBRARY RESOURCES: FINDING INFORMATION

This exercise will help you become familiar with the type of information found in many reference books.

Match the following topics with the most appropriate reference source.

_____ 1. magazine index

_____ 2. sayings about "love"

_____ 3. report on Hurricane A

_____ 4. synonyms and antonyms

_____ 5. "The Tell-Tale Heart"

_____ 6. Chicago's population

_____ 7. defines Rocky Mts.

_____ 8. synopsis of *Little Men*

_____ 9. longest hot dog

_____ 10. "Twas the night before . . ."

_____ 11. map of Antarctica

_____ 12. the stork and the fox

_____ 13. compares states

_____ 14. loan value

_____ 15. books by John Jakes

_____ 16. Missouri senators

_____ 17. general information

_____ 18. cheapest VCR

_____ 19. easily read encyclopedia

_____ 20. most-populated country

(a) *National Geographic Atlas of the World*

(b) *Official Congressional Directory*

(c) *Facts on File*

(d) *Masterplots II*

(e) *The World Almanac of the USA*

(f) *Short Story Index*

(g) *Reader's Guide to Periodical Literature*

(h) *Statistical Abstract of the United States*

(i) *N.A.D.A. Official Older Used Car Guide*

(j) *Bartlett's Familiar Quotations*

(k) *The Guinness Book of Records*

(l) *Brewer's Dictionary of Phrase and Fable*

(m) Geographical Dictionary

(n) Thesaurus

(o) *The World Book Encyclopedia*

(p) *World Almanac and Book of Facts*

(q) *The Columbia Granger's Index to Poetry*

(r) *Statistical Abstract of the World*

(s) *Contemporary Authors*

(t) *Consumer Reports Buying Guide*

Introducing Electronic Resources

Section 3 of this book introduces students to electronic resources available in school, public, and university libraries. For background information about these options, use the Using Electronic Resources handout (page 70). Following up on the introduction to Boolean logic in Section 2, use Worksheets 3A and 3B (Keyword Searching Using Boolean Logic, pages 71 and 72). The Sample Search Screen handout (page 73) shows your students how Boolean operators within keyword searches and search results may appear on their computer screens.

On-line Databases

Examples of on-line, web-based databases are listed on the handout Electronic Materials: On-line, Web-based Databases (page 74). Use this handout to introduce your students to such databases, emphasizing the different types of information found in each one. Use the handout Library Resources: Finding Information (Worksheet 3C) (page 75) to reemphasize the

importance of knowing where to find the types of information cited in the activity.

CD-ROM Databases

Examples of CD-ROM databases are listed on the handout Electronic Materials: CD-ROM Databases (page 76). Use this chart to introduce students to informational databases like these. Again, emphasize the different types of information available in each database. Next, use Library Resources: Finding Information I (Worksheet 3D) (page 77) to reemphasize the importance of knowing where to find each type of information.

Electronic Databases Review

Finally, use Worksheet 3E, Library Resources: Finding Information II (page 78) as a final review of electronic databases. At the end of this exercise, your students should be able to identify easily the major types of information found within the database.

USING
ELECTRONIC RESOURCES

Electronic Databases

Within the library, printed resources are often supplemented by on-line, web-based databases and by CD-ROM products. These electronic resources offer easy access to magazine and newspaper articles without the paper.

Electronic information is also more current information: On-line databases are often updated daily, and CD-ROM products are updated more frequently than books. Not only do you obtain more accurate information, you can also retrieve specific information without the drudgery of sorting through many printed materials. Ease of use is a major reason for the popularity of electronic resources.

Keyword Searching

Although the amount and type of magazine or newspaper articles included within each electronic database may differ, electronic resources are accessed similarly. Electronic, indexed information is represented by keywords. **Keyword searching** provides the **access point.**

Although author and title keywords are included within the electronic index, keyword searching by subject is the primary search mode. However, electronic products vary in ease. Some products utilize Library of Congress Subject Headings only. Others use Library of Congress Subject Headings, cross-referenced by keywords, in order to promote easy access. Finally, some electronic products provide a list of subject headings to help the user access information.

Using Boolean Operators

Boolean logic is often included as an option in accessing specific information. By using the

Boolean operators AND, OR, NOT, you can expand, narrow, or limit your keyword searching to find information that combines ideas. Boolean logic is particularly useful when retrieving information on a specific topic.

Retrieval Formats

Finally, electronic information can be retrieved in several formats. Most desirable is the **full-text** option, in which the actual newspaper or magazine article can be printed. Another alternative may be an **abstract**, in which only a summary of the article can be printed. **Bibliographical information**, referring the user to another full-text source, is the least desirable format.

Differences Among Databases

Although most electronic resources are designed comparably in keyword access and printing capabilities, they may differ in type and currency. On-line, web-based databases are composed of many individual databases, which are contracted through various vendors. These selected databases, updated daily, offer access to a variety of pamphlets, articles, and other reference sources. Examples of such web-based products are EBSCOhost, InfoTrac, and First Search (see handout titled "Electronic Materials: On-line, Web-based Databases").

Examples of CD-ROM databases are American Business Disc, New York Times, Academic Abstracts, and SIRS (see handout titled "Electronic Materials: CD-ROM Databases").

Name _____ Date _____

KEYWORD SEARCHING USING BOOLEAN LOGIC

> This exercise will help you find specific information using keywords and Boolean operators.

    Determine and write a keyword search command to be used for each of the reports described below. Use the Boolean operators AND, OR, and NOT to expand, narrow, or limit your keyword search.

    Example: a report comparing Mark McGwire's home runs to those of Sammy Sosa

    home runs AND Mark McGwire OR home runs AND Sammy Sosa

1. a report on recent Irish exports

    _____

    _____

2. a report on tornado damage in Kissimmee, Florida

    _____

    _____

3. a report on military buildup in the Persian Gulf

    _____

    _____

4. a report on the resolution of the United Auto Workers

    _____

    _____

5. a report on the effect of cigarette smoking on teenagers

    _____

    _____

6. a report outlining the effects of the 1997–98 El Niño on the California coast

    _____

    _____

7. a report comparing the nuclear status of Pakistan to that of India

    _____

    _____

8. a report comparing the skating performance of 1998 Olympic stars Tara Lipinski and Michelle Kwan

    _____

    _____

Name _____ Date _____

MORE KEYWORD SEARCHING USING BOOLEAN LOGIC

> This exercise will help you find specific information using keywords and Boolean operators.

Determine and write a keyword search command to be used for each of the reports described below. Use the Boolean operators AND, OR, and NOT to expand, narrow, or limit your keyword search.

Example: a report on the crime rate of all major U.S. cities, not including Chicago
crime rate AND urban cities NOT Chicago

1. a report on the black hole as cited after 1990

    _____

    _____

2. a report on all sunken ships in the twentieth century

    _____

    _____

3. a report on the total casualties of all major U.S. wars, not including the Vietnamese War

    _____

    _____

4. a report on the gradual warming effect of El Niño in the northern hemisphere

    _____

    _____

5. a report on the effects of toxic agents within the atmosphere, as relating to health problems

    _____

    _____

6. a report on unique changes in brain tissue accompanying Alzheimer's disease

    _____

    _____

7. a report comparing clothes worn in the 1940s with those worn in the 1960s, excepting shoes

    _____

    _____

SAMPLE SEARCH SCREEN

Word(s) to look for:

Along with:

Along with:

BUT NOT:

Use the following field to limit your search:

Magazine name:
Number of pages:
FULLTEXT (Y):
articles with illustrations (Y):

SAMPLE SEARCH RESULTS

SEARCH:	library use AND research	Hits: 2

Hits	Record
1.	Library Research: An Informational Quest Doe, Jane. *Library Information.* May 1998 (F7 Full Text)
2.	Exploring New Information Mediums Doe, John. *Libraries Today.* July 1998 (F7 Full Text)

F1 Help	F2 Search Screen	F4 Abstract	F6 Print

ELECTRONIC MATERIALS: ON-LINE, WEB-BASED DATABASES

EBSCOHOST	INFOTRAC	FIRST SEARCH
Sample Databases	**Sample Databases**	**General Description**
MasterFILE Elite Provides full-text access to over a thousand periodicals, and indexing and abstracts to additional periodicals; subject matter includes general reference, business, general science, health, and multicultural issues. **EBSCO Animals** Includes indexing, abstracts, and full-text information relating to animals; provides a description of familiar animals and their habitats. **Funk & Wagnalls New World Encyclopedia** Database contains over 25,000 full-text entries. **Health Source Plus** Provides full-text access for health periodicals, pamphlets, and reference books. **Newspaper Source** Provides full-text articles from United States and international newspapers.	**General Reference Center (Magazine Index)** A general interest database containing information on current events, popular culture, arts, sciences, and sports; indexes magazines, newspapers, and reference books. **Health Reference Center** A health-related database including subjects such as medicine, nutrition, fitness, pregnancy, diseases, alcohol, public health, occupational health & safety, drug abuse, and HMOs. **General BusinessFile ASAP** A business-related database to research all business and management topics; includes directory listings and investment analysis of major companies and industries.	An on-line, web-based master database composed of many general and specialized databases, indexing thousands of magazines and journals.
		Arrangement
		The databases within First Search are listed under broad categories, or database areas. Some example categories are art and humanities, business and economics, education, and life sciences. These individual databases may be generalized or specialized. They index specific titles and accompanying bibliographical information. An abstract or summary information relating to specific articles can also be accessed.
		Format
		The formats often vary from abstracts to full-text versions of magazine journal articles. Databases differ in size and in features. However, bibliographical information and library listings, specifying where the article can be found, are included within the database index. Cost of the on-line database service usually determines the amount of full text offered.
Access Points Most databases offer keyword searching with Boolean operators. Search queries can be limited to full-text articles. Magazines and publication dates can also be specified.	**Access Points** InfoTrac can be accessed as a subject guide search, keyword search, relevance ranked search, and advanced search. Search queries can be limited to full text, publication date, and journal.	**Access Points** Keyword searching is most often used to retrieve information within most databases. The keyword index specifies the desired access point (i.e., author, title searching) within most databases. The browse index provides assistance in forming the search query. Some databases also provide cross-referencing to related subject headings through the related subject feature.

Great Research Projects Step by Step

Name _____ Date _____

LIBRARY RESOURCES: FINDING INFORMATION

This exercise will help you become familiar with the type of information found in on-line, web-based databases.

You can find information for your report by using on-line, web-based databases: EBSCOhost, InfoTrac, and First Search.

Decide which of these databases is the best resource for each of the following topics. Write the name of the database next to the topic.

1. anorexia nervosa _____

2. alcohol abuse _____

3. the Siberian tiger _____

4. the World Cup _____

5. the influence of Picasso in modern art _____

6. the effects of cocaine use _____

7. multicultural recipes _____

8. general information on Pluto _____

9. downsizing in corporate America _____

10. any current event _____

11. heart disease _____

12. popular movies _____

13. a listing of major companies and industries _____

14. the most successful management style _____

15. the cat family _____

16. the rising asthma rate among children _____

17. HMOs' rising rates _____

18. a trend in education _____

 Great Research Projects Step by Step

ELECTRONIC MATERIALS: CD-ROM DATABASES

AMERICAN BUSINESS DISC	ACADEMIC ABSTRACTS	NEW YORK TIMES	SIRS
General Description American Business Disc offers specified information relating to millions of businesses in the United States. American Business Disc is used for market research and planning, sales, and business opportunities.	**General Description** An updated database, indexing magazine and journal articles published within a given time period. Covers subjects of academic and general interest.	**General Description** The New York Times database offers full-text, indexed articles that are national and international in scope. Bibliographical information relating to the individual article is included.	**General Description** SIRS Researcher and SIRS Renaissance are two SIRS databases offering full-text articles. SIRS Researcher also offers world almanac excerpts, a directory of publications, and maps of the world. SIRS Renaissance also offers award recipients related to literature and the arts, a glossary of the arts, and a list of recommended references and lifetime readings.
Arrangement The databases are arranged by company Yellow Page heading, Geography selects, Business size, and Special selects.	**Arrangement** The databases are arranged chronologically by year. The user must select the correct database to access a specific article.	**Arrangement** The databases are arranged chronologically by year. The user must select the correct database to access specific news articles.	**Arrangement** Although each article is indexed separately within the database, both SIRS databases can also be accessed through broad, topical subject headings corresponding to their printed versions. Examples of SIRS Researcher topics: education, ethnic group, family, government, and health. Examples of SIRS Renaissance topics: architecture and design, culture, film, radio, and music.
Access Points American Business Disc can be accessed through Yellow Page headings, major industry group, or SIC (Standard Industrial Code) for a geographic area.	**Access Points** The user must use keyword searching with the options of adding Boolean logic and of limiting a search query to full text.	**Access Points** The user has the option of keyword searching, using Boolean operators, or topical searching, looking through a list of alphabetically arranged, topical headings and subheadings.	**Access Points** In the SIRS Researcher, the user may access articles through subject headings, through a topic browse, or through keyword search with optional Boolean logic. SIRS Renaissance has keyword and subject headings search options, in addition to a subject tree, a hierarchal, topical listing consisting of four levels ranging from broad topics to actual articles.
Format Search for business name, address, telephone, owner/executive, size, sales volume, and credit rating.	**Format** The search concludes with a list of titles. After selecting the appropriate title, the user may access either the abstract or the full-text option, both of which include bibliographical information relating to the article.	**Format** The search results are a list of pertinent titles. After selecting a title, the user may access bibliographical information related to the article, plus the full-text article itself.	**Format** The search concludes with a list of titles. After selecting the appropriate title, the user accesses the full-text option, which includes bibliographical information related to the article.

76

Name _____ Date _____

LIBRARY RESOURCES: FINDING INFORMATION I

> This exercise will help you become familiar with the type of information found in CD-ROM databases.

You can find information for your report by using CD-ROM databases: American Business Disc, New York Times, Academic Abstracts, and SIRS.

Decide which of these databases is the best resource for each of the following topics. Write the name of the CD-ROM next to the topic.

1. a list of Newbery Award winners _____

2. employment opportunities in Earthgrain Company _____

3. ethnic groups _____

4. the death of Princess Diana _____

5. resource-based education _____

6. top-rated films _____

7. general-interest subjects _____

8. a map of Spain _____

9. the Oklahoma Federal Building bombing _____

10. secondary smoke as relating to cancer _____

11. marketing Beanie Babies _____

12. the crash of TWA flight #800 _____

13. the United Auto Workers strike in New York City _____

14. urban family life _____

15. Tony Award winners _____

16. Frank Lloyd Wright's contributions to architecture _____

17. excellence in public schools _____

Name _____ Date _____

LIBRARY RESOURCES: FINDING INFORMATION II

This exercise will help you become familiar with the type of information found in on-line, web-based databases and in CD-ROM databases.

You can find information for your report by using the following databases:

1. EBSCOhost

2. InfoTrac

3. First Search

4. American Business Disc

5. New York Times

6. Academic Abstracts

7. SIRS

Decide which of these databases is the best resource for each of the topics below. Write the number designating that database in the blank. Some numbers may be used more than once.

1. a list of Caldecott Award winners _____

2. Southwestern Bell corporate gains _____

3. the causes and treatment of bulimia _____

4. ethnic groups in the northeastern United States _____

5. charter schools _____

6. a New York ice storm _____

7. the vanishing koala bear _____

8. lowered cancer mortality rates _____

9. the physical fitness of American youth _____

10. the world's economy _____

11. a business profile on BellSouth _____

12. a directory of major companies and industries _____

SECTION 4

Researching on the Internet

Introducing the Internet

The first part of Section 4 (What Is the Internet?, pages 80–87) introduces students to the Internet and the World Wide Web and the variety of information resources they contain. Be sure your students are familiar with the components of a Web address, the purpose of search directories versus search engines, the types of search directories and engines, and the rationale for using each search feature. Use the Search Directory Comparison Chart (page 81) and Search Engine Comparison Chart (page 84) to familiarize your students with various options and their key features. Be sure each student understands the chart headings and how each search directory or engine is being compared. Use Worksheet 4A, Search Engine Exercise (page 88), to ascertain student understanding of chart terminology. An oral review of these pages is recommended.

Searching the World Wide Web

The second part of Section 4 teaches students how to begin actual Web searches. The General Searching Tips handout (page 89) lists searching procedures to follow when accessing a search engine. Be sure your students are familiar with each tip and its rationale before proceeding to student worksheets 4B through 4G, Determining Queries and Synonymous Terms, Truncation: Expanding Your Search, Search Operators: Narrowing Your Search, Designing Query Statements Using Boolean Operators and Parentheses, and Designing More Query Statements (pages 90–95). Proceed through these exercises slowly and review each exercise orally. Many students may need assistance in designing query statements with Boolean and search operators.

Web Site Analysis

The final part of Section 4 focuses on web site analysis. Select a web site, and use the form Evaluating Web Sites (page 96) as a class exercise. Discuss each criterion with your students; then reassign this chart as an individual assignment. Finally, use Locating an Inaccessible Web Site (page 97) as an oral exercise, emphasizing the importance of spelling in calling up any web site!

WHAT IS
THE INTERNET?

Although the **Internet** is a valuable research tool, some people are not sure just what it is and how it works. The Internet is a worldwide network of computer networks. It links computers together and enables information stored in one computer to become accessible to other computers. There is no one central Internet hub. Because it is a network of networks, the Internet is not dependent on any one computer in the network. One computer—in fact, hundreds of computers—could crash, and the Internet would not be affected.

The part of the Internet that most researchers are familiar with is the **World Wide Web**. This part of the Internet features millions of individual web sites offering pages with text, graphics, and hyperlinks. But that's just one part of the Internet. E-mail is also part of the Internet. So are newsgroups—discussion forums on hundreds of specialized topics. Databases of information are also part of the Internet.

With so much information on the Internet, how can you find the information you want? And how can you make sure the information is reliable?

MAKING SENSE OF THE
WORLD WIDE WEB

Many people have set out to create their own answers to these questions by trying to catalog the information on the Web. They have created search tools to help users find relevant, useful information. These search services can be divided into two main categories: **search engines** and **search directories**. Both of these services can be used to find information on the Web.

SEARCH DIRECTORIES VERSUS
SEARCH ENGINES

The terms *search directory* and *search engine* sound very similar, but they do not mean the same thing. Search directories are large data-bases of information, similar to the Yellow Pages in the telephone book, but on a larger scale. In the Yellow Pages, lists of businesses are ordered by guide words; in the search directory, the database is ordered by the layered headings and subheadings.

Search directories are located at specific web addresses, but are arranged to include other related web addresses. Search directories are composed of layered lists that are compiled by humans, not computers.

For example, suppose you wanted to find web sites with information about the history of algebra. You would first look at the main list of headings on the search directory, and choose *Education.* Clicking on *Education* will bring you a new list of headings, all relating to education. They may include choices like *Elementary, Middle School, High School,* or *College.* For algebra, you would click on *High School.* The next list of headings might include subjects taught in high school, including *Math.* Clicking on *Math* would bring you to the next level, which would probably include web sites that cover algebra. At each level of the directory, the choices you make help narrow the topic. In the example, the first topic—*Education*—was very broad. It was then narrowed down: *Education → High School → Math → Algebra.*

One of the most helpful features of search directories is that the different listings are compiled by humans. When a computer searches a database, it includes all listings that meet its search criteria, but it cannot decide whether the information is relevant to the topic. In search directories, someone has looked at each web site and decided that it includes relevant information.

To familiarize yourself with the different features of each directory, choose a topic you think you could research using this approach. Then search for the same topic on several different search directories. You will learn about the

(continued)

WHAT IS THE INTERNET? *(continued)*

types of information each site can find for you, and the strengths and weaknesses of each directory. You will also see which one is the best match for the way you think.

The chart below lists several search directories and some of their features.

SEARCH DIRECTORY COMPARISON CHART

Search Directory	Boolean Operators	Phrase Searching	Truncation	Special Features
About.com www.about.com	AND implied between words	yes, use " "	no	related search
Britannica.com www.britannica.com	AND, OR, NOT	yes, more than word searched as phrase	yes, use *	sub-searching
Galaxy www.Galaxy.com	AND implied between words; also accepts AND, OR, NOT	yes, use " "		sub-searching; metaword feature
Librarians' Index www.lii.org	AND implied between words; also accepts OR, NOT, ( )	no	yes, use *	case-sensitive metaword feature
NBCi www.nbci.com	AND, OR, AND NOT ( )	yes, use " "	no	sub-searching
Starting Point www.stpt.com	AND, OR, AND NOT, ( )	yes	no	case-sensitive; power search
The WWW Virtual Library www.vlib.org	no	no	no	sub-searching
Yahoo www.yahoo.com	no	yes, use " "	yes, use *	sub-searching; metaword feature

SEARCH ENGINES

Search engines are computer tools designed to search the Web. So when you come along to do a search, these tools function like robots reading the index terms that represent each web site and comparing them to your search term. After the search engine matches your search term with its master posting of indexing terms, it provides a list of web sites.

Unlike search directories, search engines are not preselected. Instead, search engines cover segments of the ever-changing Web in a mechanical fashion, selecting web sites related to your search term. Because search engines cover more of the Web, they are a good first choice when looking for specific subject matter.

Within the general description of "search engines," there is a lot of variety. There are many, many search engines on the Web. All of them include different pages in their indexes or databases. Although there is some overlap—some sites are indexed by a number of search engines—each search engine will probably also have sites that aren't indexed on other search engines. And all of them store and access the information in slightly different ways. Because no one search engine covers the entire World Wide Web (remember, there are probably a billion web pages out there!), it's helpful to use a variety of search engines to look for information.

(continued)

That means learning how to use the different search engines. It may help to think of search engines as being like different models of cars. All cars have some features in common: engines, seats, and wheels. But some cars also have, say, four-wheel drive; they give you much more control over the process. Some use a stick shift, and some have an automatic transmission. Some have added features, like heated seats and air conditioning. In the same way, all search engines have databases or indexes of web sites, but each search engine has its own approach to storing and retrieving sites.

USING A SEARCH ENGINE

The simplest approach to using a search engine is to type in the word you want and hit "search" (or "go," or another command). If you just want to get an idea of what kind of sites are available, this can be a useful option. But in general, it's like going to a CD megastore and saying, "I want some music." There are too many choices to be useful. In the CD store, if you just ask for music, you could spend days looking at every CD case to see if any of them look interesting. Actually checking each CD by listening to a track would take even longer. It's the same on the Internet. If you do a simple search, you can get thousands of results. Just looking at the text the search engine shows you can take a long time. Clicking on each link to check the information on the site takes even longer. What you need—in both the music store and the search engine—is a way to **focus your choices**.

In the music store, your first step in focusing the choices is to specify some musical genres. You might say, "I'm looking for some rap and hip-hop," or "I just like to listen to jazz and blues," or "I'll listen to anything except classical and country." All of these statements immediately reduce the number of choices you need to consider. You could narrow the choices down even more by being more specific: "I like classic jazz, stuff from the fifties and sixties, but just instrumentals—no vocals."

Boolean Operators

You can do the same thing in Internet searches by using something called **Boolean operators**. These are ways to limit, extend, or exclude search terms. Common Boolean operators are AND, OR, and NOT (AND NOT). The operator AND means that the word that follows must be in the text of any pages to be listed. The operator NOT (AND NOT) means that the word that follows cannot appear in any of the pages to be listed. The operator OR means that the word following may or may not be present in the pages to be listed.

Many search engines let you use Boolean operators to refine your search. Look again at the last music request above—"I like classic jazz, stuff from the fifties and sixties, but just instrumentals—no vocals." You could make the same request using Boolean operators: "jazz AND fifties OR sixties NOT vocals." A search engine that accepts Boolean operators will interpret this as meaning, "Show links to all pages that include the word *jazz* and either the word *fifties* or the word *sixties*, but leave out any links that include the word *vocals*."

If you don't use Boolean operators, or if a particular search engine doesn't support them, most search engines assume that a space between words means "and." So if you entered "jazz fifties sixties vocals," you would get only pages that included all four words. Worse yet, some search engines assume that a space between words means "or"—so you would get pages that included *any* of the words. You would probably end up with a lot of information about life in the sixties, not sixties jazz.

(continued)

WHAT IS
THE INTERNET? *(continued)*

Phrases

When talking to other people, we understand that certain words go together. To go back to the music store example, if you ask a store employee where the CD players are, the employee will understand that "CD" and "player" go together. He or she won't send you to the CD section. Unfortunately, Internet search engines aren't human. They look at each word individually—unless you tell them not to. In most search engines, the easy way to do this is to put **quotation marks** around the words you want interpreted as a phrase—in this case, "CD player." Now, instead of searching for sites that contain either *CD* or *player,* or sites that contain both *CD* and *player,* the engine will look for sites with the phrase *CD player.* This option is particularly useful if you're looking for proper names. If you're doing a project on communism and you want information about Karl Marx, you don't want to waste time on sites about the Marx Brothers.

Truncation or wildcards

The English language often has lots of variants on a word, including verb forms and plurals—as in *rap, rapper, rapping, rappers.* If you do an Internet search using just one of these forms—say, *rapper*—you will probably only get sites that include that form of the word. So if a site talks about *rappers* but never uses the word *rapper,* the search engine won't give you that site

as a result. One way to get around this is to use the search operator OR: search for rapper OR rappers. Another way is to use **truncation**, or **wildcards**. To use this option, you look for the stem of the word, and replace anything that follows the stem with an asterisk, *—a "wild card" that can take on different meanings. The search engine will then look for words that start with the stem you have included, but end in a variety of ways. If you entered the search term *rapp**, you would get results that included *rapping, rapper,* and *rappers.* However, you would also get sites that included other words beginning with *rapp*—like *rappel* and *rapport.* If you just used the stem *rap**, you might end up with sites that included words like *Raphael, rapid,* or *raptor.* For this reason, truncation works best if you can use stem words that aren't the first part of a lot of words. In the *rap* example, more words start with *rap* than with *rapp,* so *rapp* is a better choice for truncation.

Ranking results

Another feature of many search engines is that they rank results. That is, they list the results they "think" are most relevant first. Ranking criteria vary from site to site, but a higher ranking usually means a greater correlation between the search term and the content of the document.

The chart on the next page lists several search engines and some of their features.

(continued)

WHAT IS
THE INTERNET? *(continued)*

SEARCH ENGINE COMPARISON CHART

Search Engine	Boolean Operators	Phrase Searching	Truncation	Special Features	Results Ranked
Alta Vista www.altavista.com	AND, OR, AND NOT, NEAR (advanced search only)	yes, use " "	yes, use *	case-sensitive metaword feature; date range	yes, by relevance
Direct Hit www.directhit.com	no	yes	no	personalized search; related searches	yes, by rating
Excite www.excite.com	AND, OR, AND NOT	yes, use " "	no	precision search	yes, by relevance
FastSearch www.alltheweb.com	no	yes, use " "		search customization	unknown
Go.com www.go.com	no	yes	no	express search; metaword feature	yes, by rating or date
HotBot www.hotbot.com	AND, OR, NOT	yes, use " "	yes, use *	case-sensitive metaword feature	yes, by relevance
Lycos www.lycos.com	no	yes, use " "	no	advanced search	yes, by user selection; categorizes search results
Northern Light www.northernlight.com	AND, OR, NOT	yes, use " "	yes, use *	power search; metaword feature	yes, by relevance
WebCrawler www.webcrawler.com	AND, OR, NOT	yes, use " "	no	natural language queries	yes, by relevance

META SEARCH ENGINES

One interesting variation of the search engine is the **meta search engine**. *Meta* means "beyond," so a meta search engine is a more comprehensive search engine. Meta search engines search several different search engines and search directories at the same time. One advantage of this approach is that it gives a good idea of what information is available. However, meta search engines also have one big disadvantage: Because each search engine uses a slightly different syntax, the meta search engine must "translate" your query for each search engine. This makes it difficult to make a complex query through a meta search engine, because the details of your query will be lost in translation.

(continued)

WHAT IS
THE INTERNET? *(continued)*

Some useful meta search engines:

Chubba (www.chubba.com)—searches AltaVista, Excite, GoTo, Infoseek, Lycos, WebCrawler, plus others; excellent for phrases and simple searches; all searches seem to default to AND; may accept NOT. Results aggregated into one list, ranked usefully.

Dogpile (www.dogpile.com)—searches Look-Smart, GoTo, Dogpile Web Catalog, Dogpile Open Directory, Direct Hit, About.com, Info-Seek, Real Names, AltaVista, Lycos, Yahoo!, plus others. Can include Boolean operators, parentheses; not aggregated into one list.

Ixquick (www.ixquick.com)—searches AltaVista, LookSmart, Excite, Fast Search, Snap, GoTo, WebCrawler, Hotbot, Yahoo!, and more; searches engines simultaneously; translates your search into search engine's syntax; natural language or Boolean searches; supports phrases, wildcards, omitted terms, must-have terms, parentheses, NEAR; awards one star for each search engine that places a site in its top ten.

MetaCrawler (www.metacrawler.com)—searches AltaVista, Infoseek, WebCrawler, Thunderstone, Excite, Google, Lycos, LookSmart, GoTo, About.com, DirectHit, RealNames; select "ALL" for most searches; also lists pages with some of your terms (further down); accepts + to require, – to exclude; does not use Boolean operators; aggregates results based on "vote" of individual sites; can customize.

ProFusion (www.profusion.com)—searches AltaVista, InfoSeek, LookSmart, Excite, Magellan, WebCrawler, GoTo, AllTheWeb/FastSearch, Yahoo! Can customize what is searched; offers "simple", ALL terms, ANY terms, Boolean searches, modifies search to work everywhere; aggregates results into one ranked list.

RESEARCH/HOMEWORK RESOURCES

A second variation of the search engine is the research/homework resource. This type of search engine will help you look for answers to specific questions and specific research information.

Some useful research/homework resources:

AskJeeves (www.aj.com)—searches a variety of sites using natural language; phrase a question and AskJeeves looks for an answer.

Information Please (www.infoplease.com)—features on-line almanac, dictionary, and encyclopedia reference resources.

Refdesk.com (www.refdesk.com)—features reference resources, interesting daily facts, and a facts search desk.

Searchopolis (www.searchopolis.com)—searches a special collection of educational web sites; also features subsearching within a layered listing of elementary and secondary subject disciplines.

StudyWeb (www.studyweb.com)—searches research web sites; also features subsearching within a layered listing on various topics.

CNNfyi.com (www.cnnfyi.com)—features educator-designed homework materials, plus resources from education companies.

SEARCH UTILITIES

A final variant on the search engine is the downloadable search utility. These are programs that you can install on your computer. They can search your own hard drive or network, as well as the Internet. Some have free versions that you can download (www.fwnetwork.com), as well as more extensive versions that you must purchase.

(continued)

WHAT IS THE INTERNET? *(continued)*

Some useful downloadable search utilities:

Alexa (www.alexa.com) (Win, Mac)

Copernic 2000 (www.copernic.com) (Win, Mac)

EntryPoint (www.entrypoint.com) (Win, Mac)

Express Search (www.infoseekexpress.com) (Win)

GuruNet (www.gurunet.com) (Win)

Sherlock 2 (www.apple.com/sherlock) (Mac)

WebFerret (www.ferretsoft.com) (Win)

DIGITAL DOORS TO THE WORLD WIDE WEB

Web portals are "digital doors" to the World Wide Web, which have developed from search engines and indexes listed within individual web sites. These web sites offer specialized subject information, often in the form of layered databases with links to related web sites. Web portals may also include popular meta search engines or search engines that are restricted to information contained within the specialized database.

Yahoo!, Lycos, and America Online are examples of popular web portals. Other examples are listed below:

Beaucoup! (www.beaucoup.com)—searchable, specialized databases; information links

TheBigHub.com (www.thebighub.com)—specialized search categories; reference sources; weather and news

C.E.R.F.—Curriculum & Education Resource Finder (www.cerfinfo.com)—links to thousands of K–12 web sites, which are grouped by keyword, grade level, and curriculum standards

CNET Search.com (www.search.com)—searchable, specialized databases

iHaveNet.com (www.ihavenet.com)—news, information, shopping, stock quotes, search engines, and local weather

ilinkcentral.com (www.ilinkcentral.com)—weather, currency, and travel links; browsable database information

Main Portals (www.mainportals.com)—guide to the main Internet portals by subject, county, and general meta search; news; shareware

NCS: NovaNet (www.novanet.com)—an education network targeted to secondary and adult learners

Riverdeep (www.logal.net)—links to educational resources, projects, teaching tools, professional development, and news archives

Welcome to the Learning Station (www.learning-station.com)—Resource Center links to educational organizations and web sites according to discipline

(continued)

WHAT IS
THE INTERNET? *(continued)*

EVALUATING RELIABILITY

You've done a search for your topic, and you've found lots of sites with fascinating information. However, two of your sites have contradictory information. They can't both be right—but they could both be wrong. How can you tell? This is one of the biggest challenges of doing research on the Internet. Anyone with a little time and access to a computer can create a web page. The site's creator could be the world's foremost expert in the subject, or a third-grader with an imagination. You just can't believe everything you see on the Internet.

And, unfortunately, there is really no way to evaluate a site and know whether the information on it is valid or not. You need to use common sense, and some of the tools you would use to do traditional research. First of all, you should know as much as possible about the subject before you start looking on the Internet. If you already know, say, the approximate dates of the Paleozoic Era, you'll know to discount information on a site that says, "The Paleozoic Era began around 1920." If information on a web site contradicts information you already know, it's fairly likely that the web site is wrong.

One way to feel fairly confident in the information you find is to use sites you know something about. For example, the *Encyclopedia Britannica* has been an important part of most reference libraries for years. Now, much of that information is available on-line. Since the on-line version is being prepared by the same group as the print version, you can probably expect a high degree of reliability from this site. Another tried-and-true information provider is the Library of Congress. You can probably trust information you find on this site. Sites run by well-known universities are probably also good bets. The U.S. government has a number of web sites, which are generally reliable. Still, if you find something on one of these sites that just doesn't seem to make sense, trust your instincts; check the information out and try to get confirmation for it somewhere else.

The Evaluating Web Sites checklist is a useful tool to use as you investigate various sites during the research process.

Name _____   Date _____

SEARCH ENGINE EXERCISE

This exercise will help you to understand the terminology related to search engines. Use the charts (pgs. 81, 84) to provide the information requested below.

1. Name three search engines that use keyword searching. _____
    _____

2. Name three search engines that use Boolean operators in their keyword search.
    _____

3. Which search directories are especially useful for librarians? _____
    _____

4. What two search operators function within most search engines? _____
    _____

5. Why are search operators needed? _____
    _____

6. What is unique about the structure of Yahoo!? _____
    _____

7. Name two other subject directory search engines. _____
    _____

8. Why are meta search engines useful? _____
    _____

9. Name three meta search engines. _____
    _____

10. Write a command to access information for a report on California redwoods in the Northwest.
    _____

GENERAL SEARCHING TIPS

1. Try to focus your idea by defining your objective. Ask yourself what you really want to find.

2. Write down your key idea and express it in keywords. Expand your keywords into as many synonyms as possible.

3. Design your query (search statement) so that it contains at least two or three keywords.

4. Make sure your keywords represent all the information you wish to retrieve.

5. Put quotation marks around phrases or proper names.

6. Add (+) or (–) signs to words you wish to appear together or exclude within the search results.

7. Use Boolean operators AND, OR, NOT, and (AND NOT) and parentheses to specify your query. These operators must appear in ALL CAPS with a space on either side.

   AND—all documents must contain all words

   > cats AND dogs

   OR—documents may contain either word

   > cats OR dogs

   NOT—document cannot contain word

   > cats NOT dogs

   parentheses (   )—groups portions of query within Boolean search

   > cats AND (Siamese OR Persian)

   > Siamese cats or Persian cats

8. The ability to search web titles is offered through the metaword feature. Type title:word to find pages in which the specified word is contained within the web page title.

   > title:Bulimia

9. If your query does not retrieve desired information, check your search and Boolean operators. Have you placed them correctly?

10. Then examine your search query. Try rewriting it, using synonymous keywords. Add the correct operators and try again!

DETERMINING QUERIES AND SYNONYMOUS TERMS

> This exercise will help you select keywords and alternative keywords when accessing information.

A. Underline the keywords in the following questions.

1. What damage was done in the 1993 floods?

2. How rare is the white Siberian tiger?

3. How many persons have climbed Mt. Everest?

4. What is the atmosphere of Jupiter?

5. Is there life on Mars?

6. Does St.-John's-wort really cure depression?

7. Does garlic have a beneficial effect on the body?

8. Did football have its origin in Europe?

B. Place your underlined words in column #1 in the correct order. In column #2, write at least one synonym for one keyword within your query.

#1	#2
1.	
2.	
3.	
4.	
5.	
6.	
7.	
8.	

Name _____ Date _____

TRUNCATION: EXPANDING YOUR SEARCH

This exercise will help you know how to find more material when designing your search query.

When you wish to widen your search, use the * (truncation sign) to include other forms of the word in your search.

Always place the truncation sign at the end of the root syllable you wish to save. For instance, "conserva*" will gather any word having "conserva" as its root, such as "conservancy," "conservation," "conservative," and "conservatory."

A. List some of the words that may be gathered by the following truncations.

  1. president* _____

  2. appoint* _____

  3. comput* _____

  4. manager* _____

  5. automat* _____

  6. mistake* _____

  7. education* _____

  8. politic* _____

  9. informa* _____

 10. electric* _____

B. What search results could this truncated keyword gather?
    (television ad*)

_____

_____

Name _____   Date _____

SEARCH OPERATORS: NARROWING YOUR SEARCH I

This exercise will help you specify your search query so that you can find desired material.

When you wish to narrow your search by using word phrases, try the following methods:

1. Use quotation marks around words that must appear together, such as **"crime rate."**

2. Add a plus sign before a word to force its appearance in your search results list (e.g., **+juvenile+crime+rate**).

3. Add a minus sign to exclude words from a document (e.g., **+juvenile+crime+rate–adult**).

Rewrite the following **keyword phrases** according to the commands listed above.

1. Mother's Day _____

2. salt-and-pepper hair, not red _____

3. activated air bag _____

4. animal activists _____

5. Cardinal baseball statistics, not football _____

6. World Cup statistics, not dishes _____

7. French recipes _____

8. Christmas tree, not artificial _____

9. disabled American veterans _____

10. Civil War battles _____

11. chromosomal abnormalities _____

12. April Fool's Day _____

13. young drivers, not adult _____

14. unfinished furniture _____

Name _____ Date _____

SEARCH OPERATORS: NARROWING YOUR SEARCH II

This exercise will help you specify your search query so that you can find desired material.

When you wish to narrow your search by using word phrases, try the following methods:

1. Use quotation marks around words that must appear together, such as **"crime rate."**

2. Add a plus sign before a word to force its appearance in your search results list (e.g., **+juvenile+crime+rate**).

3. Add a minus sign to exclude words from a document (e.g., **+juvenile+crime+rate–adult**).

Rewrite the following **keyword phrases** according to the commands listed above.

1. Happy Birthday _____

2. miniature golf course _____

3. rising crime rate _____

4. Three Musketeers, not candy _____

5. Windows, not glass _____

6. Pulitzer Prize winner _____

7. Ronald Reagan _____

8. All-Star Game _____

9. Hall of Fame, not football _____

10. Apollo, not god _____

11. Hershey, Pennsylvania, not candy _____

12. higher education _____

13. red, white, and blue _____

14. Lake Michigan _____

Name _____   Date _____

DESIGNING QUERY STATEMENTS USING BOOLEAN OPERATORS AND PARENTHESES

This exercise will help you specify your search query so that you can find desired material.

Write a query statement to find information for the topics below. Use Boolean operators **AND**, **OR**, and **NOT** (or **AND NOT**), including parentheses, to specify query statements.

Example: **music AND (rock OR classic)**   **rock music or classic music**

1. sports equipment, may include football, baseball, but not basketball

   _____

2. roast beef, ham, steak entrees with chocolate cake, apple pie

   _____

3. Coke, iced tea, milk with hamburgers, hot dogs, bratwurst

   _____

4. Native American culture, especially Cherokee, Sioux, Seneca, but not Mohawk

   _____

5. hitting record of Babe Ruth, Ty Cobb, Willie Mays

   _____

6. Persian Gulf War casualties, except for reserve units

   _____

7. temperature, humidity for Chicago, Detroit, St. Louis, but not New York City

   _____

8. benefits of eyeglasses vs. soft contacts

   _____

Name _____ Date _____

DESIGNING MORE QUERY STATEMENTS

This exercise will help you specify your search query so that you can find desired material.

Write a query to find information for the topics below. Add quotation marks, search operators (+), (–), and Boolean operators **AND**, **OR**, **NOT** (or **AND NOT**), including parentheses, to specify query statements. (Hint: Many queries can be written more than one way.)

1. French recipes, not American

   _____

2. rules of baseball, may have football as an alternative

   _____

3. symptoms of leprosy, including death rate

   _____

4. 1980s fashions

   _____

5. damage caused by Hurricane Camille in Mississippi

   _____

6. Dutch Elm disease in American trees

   _____

7. tall buildings, may include Empire State Building, John Hancock Tower, Sears Tower

   _____

8. statistics of American League teams including Detroit Lions, Oakland Athletics, not Cleveland Indians

   _____

9. futuristic cars 2030–2050

   _____

Name _____   Date _____

EVALUATING
WEB SITES

_____

Name of Site _____

URL _____

Checklist Items	Yes	No
CONTENT		
Does the subject matter fit search term?		
Is the information relevant to search term?		
Does the information appear comprehensive?		
Do graphics enhance content?		
ORGANIZATION		
Does the web site have a defined purpose?		
Is information written clearly?		
Is information well organized?		
Does web site have an outline or table of contents?		
Does web site provide links to web sites containing related subject matter?		
AUTHORITY		
Is the author noted on the web site?		
Is the author's background information noted?		
When was the web site constructed?		
When was the web site last updated?		
Does the webmaster request feedback for improvement?		
RELIABILITY		
Is the content free from bias?		
Are sources of information cited within the web site?		
Is the web site supported by agencies/institutions?		

Name _____   Date _____

LOCATING AN INACCESSIBLE WEB SITE

The following tips may be helpful in reaching web sites:

> 1. Make sure your web address is correct. Even one small mistake in spelling or in punctuation will prevent access.
>
> 2. If you have keyed in the correct address, but cannot access the web page, try keying in the domain name to access the home page. Then access hyperlinks to reach your desired web site.

The following web addresses cannot be accessed. Reduce the web address to its domain name. Look at the subdirectories and try to determine which hyperlinks will lead you to the desired web site.

Example: **http://www.interstateauto.com/museums/iowa.index.html**
domain name: (www.interstateauto.com)
hyperlinks: museums, Iowa

1. http://www.prospernet.com/surfing/recreation/automotive

   domain name: _____

   hyperlinks: _____

2. http://www.toolcity.net/cars/modela.html

   domain name: _____

   hyperlinks: _____

3. http://www.ucr.edu/car/museumtrans.html

   domain name: _____

   hyperlinks: _____

4. http://www.bios.niu.edu/orion/conlist.html

   domain name: _____

   hyperlinks: _____

5. http://www.aminews.com/ski/index/colorado/

   domain name: _____

   hyperlinks: _____

SECTION 5

Using Original Source Material

Introducing Primary Resources

Section 5 begins with an introduction to primary resources in general and to primary-source, electronic media in particular (Original or Primary Sources, page 100). These pages reinforce the idea of primary resources as original experiences. Use the General Netiquette Rules handout (page 101) to establish proper conduct (etiquette) associated with electronic media: e-mail, listservs, chat groups, and newsgroups. Use the Electronic Mail handout (page 102) as an overview for e-mail. The handout Listservs, Chat Groups, and Newsgroups (page 103) is designed to introduce these media as potential primary-source, electronic resources. To teach these media most effectively, access some of the sample listserv and newsgroup sites listed in the handout. Instead of demonstrating chat room conversation, you may simply wish to emphasize to your students that the value of a chat group as primary-source material depends upon the caliber of the conversation! After your demonstration, use Worksheet 5A, Electronic Communications Exercise (page 104), to review the characteristics of each electronic medium.

Other Primary-source Materials

The concluding portion of Section 5 introduces students to other primary-source materi-als. Use the Interlibrary Loan handout (page 105) to teach students how to obtain out-of-print books.

Use the Interviews and Tips for Conducting a Successful Interview handouts (pages 106, 107) as guidelines for conducting an interview. Then ask your students to conduct a five-minute interview, via e-mail or in person. Distribute the E-mail/Interview Planning Sheet (Worksheet 5B) (page 108), requesting that each student list appropriate interview questions. After the questions have been checked, you can permit the interview to take place. *If you opt for a personal interview, make sure that students record their conversations.* Immediately after the interview has been conducted, have students use Worksheet 5C, Transcribing the Interview (page 109), to ensure that their interview material is accurately recorded.

Next, introduce diaries and journals as valuable primary sources. Use the Diaries and Journals handout (page 110) to introduce the value of personal experiences as information sources through an example journal entry. Finally, use the handout Art Forms, Music Forms, and Realia (page 111) to show students that these resources can also be a means of conveying the past to the present.

ORIGINAL, OR PRIMARY, SOURCES

Primary sources make library research come alive. Projects based on firsthand accounts portray subject matter more accurately. Like meals topped off with dessert, these projects are more complete.

Types of Primary Sources

Primary sources recount original experiences. They exist in many forms. Electronic media include **e-mail**, **listservs**, **chat groups**, and **newsgroups**, in which personal experiences are communicated. **Interviews** are also valuable primary sources. **Diaries** and **published journals** often portray events from the author's perspective. They are often used by researchers to analyze a subject's thoughts, ideas, beliefs, motives, and character traits in an effort to explain the subject's actions. Finally, **art** and **music forms** and **realia** (personal objects), taken from the time of the event, convey prevailing attitude and mood. They also disclose the owner's personal taste and reveal conventional customs and mores.

Using Primary Sources to Add Credibility

Within the research project, primary sources should be used whenever possible. As original evidence, firsthand accounts authenticate an assertion (position) made within the thesis, adding credibility to the entire statement.

Using Primary Sources to Provide Documentation

Primary sources can also provide documentation for all supports within the thesis statement. For instance, an interview with Mark McGwire could provide both the supports and the evidence for the position that McGwire's ability to hit 70 homeruns during a single season was due to whatever reason he states!

As you plan your research project, try to add as many primary sources as possible. As original evidence, firsthand accounts will add an exciting dimension to your research project, making it come alive!

GENERAL NETIQUETTE RULES

1. **Investigate cyberspace.** Be sure to select the electronic medium appropriate for the subject you wish to discuss.

2. **Be careful.** Do not reveal personal information. Stop "conversations" that make you uncomfortable.

3. **Be polite.** Electronic communication, although faceless, should be businesslike and polite.

   (a) Do not use rude, objectionable, or offensive language.

   (b) Do not harass another user.

   (c) Do not send heated, or emotional, messages ("flames").

   (d) Do not "shout" by using all uppercase letters.

   (e) Do not dominate group "conversations." Send messages that are appropriately targeted to the conversation subject.

   (f) Do not reproduce electronic messages that you have received without the sender's permission. Copyright laws protect e-mail.

4. **Do not send private messages.** Electronic communication is not confidential.

5. **Keep your messages short and specific.** Clarify your messages by using subject headings whenever possible and by including your signature.

ELECTRONIC MAIL

Electronic mail consists of messages transmitted through networks by mail protocol. Electronic mail is routed through networks by its **e-mail address**, which names its final destination. An e-mail address names its recipient by including the **user's name** or **user id**, plus the **domain name** of the hub: the computer or server acting as the post office.

Example: **johndoe@more.connect.more.net**

Incoming electronic mail is retrieved from the post office by computer software, which allows the user to read and to respond to mail.

Electronic mail is easy to read. The mail header contains the e-mail address of the recipient (To:), the sender's address (From:), and the subject of the message (Subject:). The message appears in letter form.

E-mail, as an Internet application, is available through service providers. Free e-mail sites are offered through web sites such as:

Hotmail (www.hotmail.com)
CollegeClub.com (www.collegeclub.com)
World Email Directory (www.worldemail.com)

E-mail has no national registry. A few specialized services, referred to as **white pages**, exist. The following web sites may be used as directories:

people.yahoo.com
www.worldemail.com

E-mail can be an excellent primary information source, particularly when messages describe firsthand experiences.

LISTSERVS, CHAT GROUPS, AND NEWSGROUPS

	Listservs	Chat Groups	Newsgroups
Definition	A listserv is an Internet discussion group delivered through electronic mail. A listserv is made up of a list of subscribers who interact by sending e-mail messages.	International Relay Chat (IRC) is a system for connecting Internet users at real time for the purpose of exchanging messages. These networked group discussions are referred to as chat.	Newsgroups are sets of people who exchange subject-related discussions over a network. Local and global newsgroups are defined and named by their subject matter.
Structure	Listservs may be moderated by operators, who screen messages for content. Listservs are implemented and maintained by mail servers, which automatically forward e-mail messages to the list of e-mail subscribers.	IRC is accessed through computer software and is maintained by global IRC networks. IRC on-line exchanges are organized by channels. Most channels have a name and topic. Users can either join these channels or create new channels.	Global newsgroups are often part of a set of newsgroups referred to as **Usenet**. Usenet newsgroups are arranged in an hierarchical structure. Some of the broad categories are listed below: **comp:** computer-related **sci:** science-related **soc:** social issues **talk:** talk **news:** network news **misc:** other topics **rec:** recreation **humanities:** fine arts/literature
Content	Listservs exist on a wide variety of specified topics. Listserv addresses may be retrieved by topic (subject) through search engines and directory lists located at the following web sites: **www.liszt.com** (mailing lists) or **http://galaxy.einet.net/ GJ/lists.html**.	Variable; user-determined.	Specific newsgroups are identified by subcategories, separated by periods (e.g., rec.sports. soccer). The identity of specific newsgroups depends upon the willingness of its users to maintain pertinent discussions. Some newsgroups are moderated. In general, newsgroups are defined by the type of news items posted.
Access	Interested subscribers may join a listserv by e-mailing the following request to the **listserv address: subscribe listname your name**. Subscribers can drop a listserv by e-mailing the following request to the **listserv address: signoff listname**. *	Users may choose a nickname and must start an IRC session with the **"/Nick"** command. Basic IRC commands beginning with a "/" must be observed. Channels are managed by a channel operator (chan-op), whose operating privileges may be transferred to a new user.	To find newsgroups discussing a specific topic, use one of the **Web Usenet search tools: www.dejanews.com** or **www.liszt.com**.
Value	Listservs, as forums for targeted, subject-related exchanges, can be valuable primary information sources.	Users must observe general netiquette rules while exchanging conversation. The quality of the chat depends upon its participants. The value of a chat group as a primary source of information depends upon its discourse.	The value of a newsgroup as a primary source of information depends upon the value of the firsthand experiences discussed.

* The **listname** within both commands refers to the name of the listserv.

ELECTRONIC COMMUNICATIONS EXERCISE

This exercise will help you better understand electronic communication media.

Match the correct electronic communication medium listed below with the numbered characteristics that follow.

(a) E-mail　　　　　　　　(c) Chat groups (IRC)

(b) Listservs　　　　　　　(d) Newsgroup

_____ 1. arranged hierarchically

_____ 2. listed in "white pages"

_____ 3. reproduced in a listing

_____ 4. exchanged through channels

_____ 5. join by subscribing

_____ 6. may use a nickname

_____ 7. may be retrieved through search engines or directory list

_____ 8. commands begin with "/"

_____ 9. hot mail

_____ 10. named by the subject it discusses

_____ 11. forwards e-mail messages

_____ 12. an Internet application

_____ 13. arranged in eight broad categories

_____ 14. operates in real time

_____ 15. chan-op

_____ 16. signoff list name

INTERLIBRARY LOAN

Interlibrary Loan (ILL) is a borrowing service between networks of cooperating libraries. Member university and public libraries usually form separate networks, participating in partnerships with other university and public libraries to provide requested library materials to their patrons.

Interlibrary Loan can help you obtain reproductions of original-source materials not held within your local library. Requests may include reproductions of old documents or copies of books no longer in print.

The **interlibrary loan form** shown below is used by public libraries to lend specific library materials to an individual patron. Materials may be requested from branches within a public library district or from other public library districts.

ONLY ONE TITLE PER FORM, PLEASE

DEWEY #:	❏ JUVENILE ❏ ADULT
AUTHOR:	

TITLE (or SUBJECT):	EDITION:
	SUBSTITUTE ❏ Y ❏ N

TODAY'S DATE:	NOT WANTED AFTER:
YOUR NAME:	
DAYTIME PHONE #:	EVENING PHONE #:

Patron must give full name & address on the reverse side.

IF ITEM IS NOT AVAILABLE IN OUR DISTRICT, HOW MUCH ARE YOU WILLING TO PAY TO RECEIVE IT BY INTERLIBRARY LOAN?	STAFF USE ONLY
❏ NONE ❏ $10.00 ❏ $5.00 ❏ ANY COST ❏ OTHER COST _____	STAFF INITIALS
	PATRON CALLED:
	PB #

(THIS SIDE FOR LIBRARY STAFF USE ONLY)
OWNING BRANCHES

❏ KL _____ (_)	❏ KR _____ (_)
❏ SP _____ (_)	❏ MY _____ (_)
❏ MK _____ (_)	❏ NC _____ (_)
❏ CP _____ (_)	❏ SC _____ (_)
❏ DR _____ (_)	❏ BT _____ (_)

PUBLISHER:	ADDITIONAL INFORMATION:
ISBN:	
PUB. DATE:	
ON ORDER? ❏ YES ❏ NO	

REQUESTING BRANCH	SEND ILL: ❏ YES ❏ NO
❏ KL ❏ DR ❏ SC ❏ SP ❏ KR ❏ BT ❏ MK ❏ MY ❏ CP ❏ NC	MCAT ❏ YES ❏ NO LC #
	BIP + ❏ YES ❏ NO BTLINK ❏ YES ❏ NO

ILL9709–1.2

INTERVIEWS

Eyewitness Accounts

An interview is an important way to find an eyewitness account of an incident or event to validate the thesis statement. Of course, it is important to choose the right person to report the information desired. For example, a World War II veteran who took part in the Normandy invasion would be an excellent resource to support the position that World War II combat was difficult. On the other hand, his wife, who lived during the war but did not take part in combat, would not be a good original source to support this particular thesis.

Interviews are appropriate when the respondent (the person being interviewed) can provide authentic evidence that relates to the thesis statement. The best respondent will be an ordinary person who witnessed a unique event.

Biographical Information

Interviews are also appropriate when the respondent can provide detailed biographical information related to the thesis statement. For example, a thesis statement attributing personal bankruptcy as the motivation that led a businessperson to start three successful corporations is best documented by interviewing that particular individual. Occasionally, the life of an ordinary person may illustrate a success story or serve as a case history, but in most instances, interviewers look for people who lived unusual lives or accomplished extraordinary things.

Discussions of Techniques

Finally, interviews are appropriate when the respondent discusses techniques or methods included in the thesis statement. For example, an interview with athlete Tiger Woods on golfing techniques would provide exciting supportive evidence for a thesis statement related to golf. Other interesting interviews might include celebrities, such as artists, musicians, and other performers.

Creating Interview Questions

After selecting the respondent, you must decide exactly what information is needed, then design interview questions that will enable you to collect the desired information.

The interview questions must be clearly related to the purpose of the interview. All questions must be worded concisely. Because the interview is intrusive, the interviewer should only ask questions that solicit specific, objective answers. The respondent may include feelings and attitudes in the answer, but the interviewer should not deliberately seek these responses. Personal questions should never be asked.

You should give the respondent a list of questions before the interview. Here are some examples of appropriate interview questions:

1. What were three memorable events in your childhood?
2. Name the single greatest factor of your success.
3. What is the highlight of your career?

TIPS FOR CONDUCTING A SUCCESSFUL INTERVIEW

Because a taped interview is an intrusion upon another person's time, the interview session should be regarded as a privilege. The following tips are crucial for conducting a successful interview.

1. **Be targeted.** Know your information objective.

2. **Be selective.** Determine exactly the type of information needed and find out which person has the background and expertise to supply the desired information. Ask that person.

3. **Be courteous.** Make arrangements to meet before the interview.

4. **Be prepared.** Formulate your questions in advance. Clearly state them and write them down. Make sure your tape recorder works properly. Don't forget your tape!

5. **Be specific.** If you desire specific information, design your questions accordingly. Ask for objective information.

6. **Be focused.** Keep the conversation directed to the question. Politely steer away from irrelevant comments.

7. **Be limited.** Restrict your interview to 30 minutes. Remember: The shorter the interview, the shorter the transcription!

Name _____ Date _____

E-MAIL/INTERVIEW PLANNING SHEET

Interviewer:	
Respondent:	
Subject to Be Discussed:	

QUESTIONS

1. _____
   _____

2. _____
   _____

3. _____
   _____

4. _____
   _____

5. _____
   _____

6. _____
   _____

7. _____
   _____

8. _____
   _____

■■

Teacher comments: _____
_____

Name _____ Date _____

TRANSCRIBING
THE INTERVIEW

Transcription	Notes

DIARIES AND JOURNALS

Explanations for Individual Actions

Diaries and journals are private accounts of incidents and events occurring within one's life. Because they are personal accounts, diary and journal entries reveal personality, opinions, and feelings. As primary information sources, they offer explanation for individual actions.

Private diaries and journals comment on events and occurrences from an individual perspective. Through these remarks, past political ideologies and social mores slowly emerge, painting past society in microcosm.

Uses in Research

Diaries and journals are often used by researchers as source material to determine personality traits, to determine causes for individual acts, to re-create past life, to define outstanding historical events, and to describe individual, regional, and national viewpoints. Family diaries are not always available. If one is unavailable to you, check your local library archives or the Library of Congress web site (www.loc.gov) for firsthand accounts.

A Sample Diary Entry

The journal entry below was written by my then 15-year-old uncle in 1930, shortly after immigrating from Holland to the United States. My uncle's youthful optimism is obvious in his comments.

OUR BEING IN AMERICA

One thing we like about this country is there are so many hills and woods. This we do not have in our country.

We are very glad we came here and like this country very much. School is not hard here, like it is in the Netherlands. Skipping school is something we learned to do here and I at first brought this in practice very much. I usually then went to the library and took books home. Once I skipped twelve times without anybody knowing it.

The winters here are much colder than in Holland and the summer is much warmer.

ART FORMS, MUSIC FORMS, AND REALIA

Art Forms

Art forms, such as original paintings and sculptures, are not considered part of most library collections. They are usually found in art museums and special art libraries. The art forms most often found in library holdings are an occasional collection of original photographs included within local genealogical records. These photographs and accompanying records are excellent primary resources in understanding local history.

Music Forms

Similarly, original **music forms** are usually found within specialized collections. However, taped or CD versions of original music forms have become popular additions to many library collections. For the most part, these music holdings are only variations of the original piece, but occasionally, some music selections simulate the primary resource, playing the original piece on authentic instruments. These "primary resources" are valuable in understanding the emotions and moods of specific eras.

Realia

Realia (personal objects) are not part of most library collections, but may be added to the library research project. Realia may include family heirlooms: antiques, clothing, personal objects, and artifacts (such as native American arrowheads). Realia may be gathered from family members and acquaintances, from searches (such as fossil hunts or archeological digs), or from private antique dealers.

Realia bring the past to the present. Within the thesis statement, realia documents support evidence, strengthening its overall position. By adding external appeal, realia enrich print.

SECTION 6

Interesting Web Sites

Teacher Guide Page

Section 6 presents an overview of topical Internet resources. Each of the 18 topics lists web sites suitable for research projects. Subject disciplines pertaining to each topic are also cited.

To use these lists effectively, you must make sure that students have first planned their research projects. Then, after selecting the appropriate topical list(s), they should investigate the referenced web sites to narrow their topics and to establish whether sufficient background knowledge is cited. Next, from the information found at these web sites, they should define the parameters of their projects—with your approval—according to their individual abilities.

After you have determined and approved the objectives of each research project, students can begin the research process.

Depending upon the skill level of your students, you may choose to have them begin with a short assignment rather than a large project. (For example, ask each student to find out the level of education, job requirements, and starting salary of his or her prospective occupation.) As you become more familiar with these lists and students gain confidence in their research techniques, you can plan larger research projects. The general reference source list also will help your researchers find more specialized information.

These topical lists are not comprehensive, but are intended as springboards for further investigation. Feel free to add your own additions and other changes as time goes on. No one can ever find all the information available on the Web; therefore, encourage your students to keep searching!

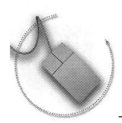

WEB SITES TO INVESTIGATE DURING THE RESEARCH PROCESS

AMERICAN NATIONAL PARKS

www.karinya.com/amntpks.htm
American National Park Scenes

www.areaparks.com
Area Parks Network for United States Parks

www.webdirectory.com/Parks_and_Recreation/
Environmental Organization Web Directory

www.gorp.com
GORP.com

www.halcyon.com/rdpayne/
National Parks and Monuments of the
Pacific Northwest

www.npca.org
National Parks and Conservation Association
Home Page

www.nps.gov
ParkNet: The National Park Service

www.yahoo.com
Yahoo—search "national parks"

Subject Disciplines:

Language Arts/English
Science
Social Studies/History

AMERICAN POETS

www.poets.org/index.cfm
The Academy of American Poets

www.bucks.edu/library/lib_resource/
ampoetsa.htm
American Poets and Poetry on the Internet

www.yahoo.com/promotions/poet/
April Is National Poetry Month!

www.bartleby.com
Bartleby.com: Great Books Online

www.hti.umich.edu/english/amverse/
HTI American Verse Project

www.poets.com
Hall of Fame

www.poetry.com
Poetry.Com

www.poems.com/archive.htm
Poetry Archive

www.poetrysociety.org
Poetry Society of America

Subject Disciplines:

Language Arts/English
Multicultural Studies

THE AMERICAN PRESIDENTS

www.grolier.com/presidents/preshome.html
The American Presidency

www.americanpresidents.org
American Presidents: Life Portraits

www.historyplace.com
The History Place

www.ipl.org/ref/POTUS
IPL POTUS–Presidents of the United States

www.seanet.com/users/pamur/ahistory.html
The Time Page: American History Sites

www.whitehouse.gov
Welcome to the White House

Subject Disciplines:

Language Arts/English
Social Studies/History

(continued)

WEB SITES TO INVESTIGATE DURING THE RESEARCH PROCESS

(continued)

CAREERS

www.aip.org/careers/
    AIP Career Services Home Page

www.ajb.dni.us
    America's Job Bank

www.bls.gov
    BLS (Bureau of Labor Statistics) Home Page

www.careerbabe.com
    CareerBabe

www.career-index.com
    Career-Index.com

www.careerzone-uk.com
    Career Information

www.careerkey.com
    Jobs, careers

www.jobbankusa.com
    Job Search

www.healthcareerweb.com
    HealthCareerWeb

www.jobprofiles.com
    Job Profiles.com

www.jobweb.com
www.jobweb.org
    JobWeb

www.gordonworks.com
    Jobs, Careers, Employment, and Job Search

www.ams.org/careers
    Mathematical Sciences Career Information

www.minorities-jb.com
    Welcome to Minorities' Job Bank

Subject Disciplines:

Language Arts
Social Studies

CLASSIC AND ANTIQUE CARS

www.autoracemuseum.com
    Auto Race Museum Home

www.carcollector.com
    Car Collector Magazine

www.car-stuff.com
    Car-Stuff

www.hemmings.com
    Hemmings Motor News

www.ucr.edu/h-gig/hist-art/mustrans.html
    History Museum Links – Transportation

www.toolcity.net/~robt/modela.html
    The Intrigue of "Henry's Lady"

www.kruseinternational.com
    Kruse International (links)

www.motorlit.com
    MotorLit.com

www.classicar.com
    World Wide Wheels Classified

Subject Disciplines:

Art
Language Arts/English
Social Studies

CONSTELLATIONS

www.slivoski.com/astronomy/
    Amateur Astronomy

www.dibonsmith.com
    The Constellations Web Page

liftoff.msfc.nasa.gov
    Liftoff to Space Education

(continued)

WEB SITES TO INVESTIGATE DURING THE RESEARCH PROCESS

(continued)

www.bios.niu.edu/orion/conlist.html
 List of Constellations

www.nasa.gov
 NASA Homepage (Space Science Link)

www.astronomical.org
 Peoria Astronomical Society

www.astro.wisc.edu/~dolan/constellations/
constellations.html
 Stars and Constellations

www.seds.org
 Students for the Exploration and
 Development of Space

www.windows.ucar.edu
 Introduction to Windows to the Universe

www.windows.umich.edu/the_universe/the_
universe.html
 The Universe

Subject Disciplines:

Language Arts/English
Science
Social Studies

ENDANGERED SPECIES

www.audubon.org
 Audubon Online

www.awesomelibrary.org
 The Awesome Library
 search "endangered species"

www.bagheera.com
 BAGHEERA

www.louisville.edu/library/ekstrom/govpubs/
subjects/endangered/endangered.html
 Endangered and Protected Species

www.endangeredspecie.com
 EndangeredSpecie.com: The Rarest Info
 Around

www.iwc.org
 International Wildlife Coalition

www.newhorizons.org/gng_species.html
 Outside the Building: Ground and Gardens:
 Endangered Species

www.fws.gov
 US Fish & Wildlife Service Home Page
 (Endangered Species)

www.wwf.org
 WWF– US: World Wildlife Fund

Subject Disciplines:

Art
Science
Social Studies/History

FAMOUS AMERICAN ARTISTS

www.usc.edu/isd/archives/ethnicstudies/
africanamerican/black_art.html
 African American Artists

www.artists4a.com
 The Alliance of African-American Artists

www.aldrin.org
 Anders Aldrin Online Gallery

www.artcyclopedia.com
 Artcyclopedia

www.artseek.com/ArtSites/museums.html
 ArtSeek – museums

www.egallery.com/jazz.html
 The Electric Gallery: The Jazz and Blue Wing

www.mfa.org
 Museum of Fine Arts

www.nmaa.si.edu
 Smithsonian American Art Museum

www.tfaoi.com
 TFAOI.com

www.artnet.com
 Welcome to artnet.com

www.echonyc.com/~whitney/
 Whitney Museum of American Art

(continued)

WEB SITES TO INVESTIGATE DURING THE RESEARCH PROCESS

(continued)

www.wbgallery.com
   Wilson Brown Gallery

Subject Disciplines:

Art
Multicultural Studies

MUMMIES

www.tlc.discovery.com
   TLC
   search "Mummies in the Mist"

www.totentanz.de/mummies.htm
   Mummies

www.verdenet.com/isis/mummy.htm
   Mummies

www.pbs.org/wgbh/nova/
   (Previous Sites)
   Nova Online: Ice Mummies of the Inca

www.pbs.org/wgbh/nova/
   (Previous Sites)
   Nova Online: Mysterious Mummies of China

Subject Disciplines:

Science
Social Studies/History

NATIVE AMERICAN CULTURE

www.adobe-east.com
   AdobeEast (Links)

www.americanwest.com/pages/indians.htm
   The American West – Native Americans

www.thewildwest.org
   CyberSoup's The Wild West

www.heard.org
   The Heard Museum

www.artnatam.com
   ArtNatAm: Native American Art Exhibit

www.ed.uri.edu/smart/homepage/indians.htm
   Native Americans

www.learningspace.org/instruct/high_school/
sites/nat_amer.html
   Native Americans

www.nativeweb.org
   NativeWeb

Subject Disciplines:

Art
Language Arts/English
Music
Multicultural Studies
Social Studies/History

THE OLD AMERICAN WEST

www.americanwest.com
   The America's West (Links)

www.miningco.com
   About – The Human Internet
   search "American West"

www.historybuff.com/library/index.html
   History Buff's Reference Library
   Old West

www.virtualwest.com/trivia/
   An Old West Trivia Game

www.over-land.com
   The Overland Trail (Links)

www.linecamp.com
   Stage Coach into American History Museums

www.pbs.org/weta/thewest/
   New Perspectives on the West

www.gunslinger.com/west.html
   The Wild Wild West

Subject Disciplines:

Language Arts/English
Social Studies/History

(continued)

WEB SITES TO INVESTIGATE DURING THE RESEARCH PROCESS

(continued)

ROCKS AND MINERALS

www.enchantedrocks.com
  Amethyst, rose quartz . . .

agcwww.bio.ns.ca/indexe.html
  (Educational Resources)
  Geological Survey of Canada

www.uky.edu/KGS/coal/webrokmn/rocksmin.htm
  Rocks and Minerals of Kentucky

www.marinmineral.com
  Marin Mineral Company

www.minerals.net
  The Mineral and Gemstone Kingdom

www.galleries.com
  (Mineralogical Data)
  The Mineral Gallery

www.rocksandminerals.com
  Rockmans Rocks, Minerals and Fossils (Links)

Subject Disciplines:

Science

SNOW SPORTS

www.adventureteam.com
  Adventure Team USA

www.itsnet.com/home/getlost/fun.html
  Get Lost Sports and Recreation

www.goski.com
  GoSki.com

www.gorp.com
  GORP– Great Outdoor Recreation Pages

www.hyperski.com/index.htm
  Hyperski

www.aminews.com
  OnTheSnow.com

skicentral.com
  Ski Central –Skiing and Snowboarding Index and Search

www.skidirectory.com
  Ski Directory: The Winter Sports Search Engine

www.yahoo.com/Recreation/Sports/Snowboarding/
  Snowboarding

www.snowlink.com
  SnowLink

www.olympic-usa.org
  United States Olympic Committee

Subject Disciplines:

Physical Education
Science
Social Studies

UNITED STATES—STATES

fermi.jhuapl.edu/states
  Color Landform Atlas of the United States

www.nationalgeographic.com
  NATIONALGEOGRAPHIC.COM (Maps)

www.census.gov/datamap/www/
  State and County Demographic and Economic Profiles

www.piperinfo.com/state/states.html
  State and Local Government on the Net

www.lcweb.loc.gov/global/state/stategov.html
  State and Local Governments (Library of Congress)

www.csg.org
  States News

www.usahistory.com
  United States History presidents and statistics

www.historyoftheworld.com/usa/ushist.htm
  The United States Links Page

www.infoplease.com/states.html
  U.S. States

(continued)

WEB SITES TO INVESTIGATE DURING THE RESEARCH PROCESS

(continued)

Subject Disciplines:

Language Arts/English
Social Studies/History

THE UNEXPLAINED AND MYSTERIOUS

www.atlan.org
  Atlantis—The Lost Continent Finally Found

www.activemind.com
  Mysterious and Unexplained
  Atlantis

www.crystalinks.com/loch_ness.html
  Loch Ness Monster

www.wsu.edu/~delahoyd/monsters.html
  Monsters

www.lochness.co.uk
  Nessie on the Net

www.pbs.org/wgbh/nova/
  (Previous Sites)
  Nova Online: The Beast of Loch Ness

www.amherst.edu/~ermace/sth/sth.html
  Stonehenge (Links)

www.activemind.com
  Mysterious and Unexplained
  Stonehenge

dir.yahoo.com/Science/Alternative/
Paranormal_Phenomena/Ancient_
Civilizations/
  Yahoo!

Subject Disciplines:

Language Arts/English
Science
Social Studies/History

UNITED STATES CIVIL WAR BATTLES

www.civilwarhome.com
  The American Civil War Home Page

www.americancivilwar.com
  The American Civil War Map Exhibits

memory.loc.gov
  American Memory—Front Door

www.civil-war.net/battles.html
  The Civil War Home Page

homepages.dsu.edu/jankej/civilwar/civilwar.htm
  Civil War Index Page

metalab.unc.edu/docsouth/
  Documenting the American South

www.libs.uga.edu/darchive/hargrett.html
  Hargrett Library Digital Archive

www.loc.gov
  Libary of Congress

www.cwc.lsu.edu
  The United States Civil War Center

jefferson.village.virginia.edu/vshadow/
  The Valley of the Shadow Contents

Subject Disciplines:

Language Arts/English
Social Studies

WATER SPORTS

www.aqueous.com
  Aqueous.com

www.main.org/cawsc/
  Capital Area Water Ski Club

www.cbs.sportsline.com
  CBS Sportsline

www.espn.com
  ESPN.com

www.h2opolo.com
  H2O Polo (Links)

www.showski.com
  National Show Ski Association

www.scubabob.com
  SCUBA DIVING

(continued)

WEB SITES TO INVESTIGATE DURING THE RESEARCH PROCESS

(continued)

www.sportingnews.com
  The Sporting News

www.cnnsi.com
  CNN Sports Illustrated

www.waterski.ca
  Water Ski Canada

Subject Disciplines:

Physical Education
Social Studies

WILDFLOWERS

www.nps.gov/plants/cw/
  Celebrating Wildflowers

www.dfwalmanac.com/wildflowers/
  Dallas/Ft. Worth Wildflowers

www.gardenweb.com
  (Glossary of Botanical Terms)
  GardenWeb Home Page

www.wildflower.org
  Lady Bird Johnson Wildflower Center

www.nps.gov/plants/
  Plant Conservation Alliance

www.wild-flowers.com
  Wildflowers

aggie-horticulture.tamu.edu/wildseed/
wildflowers.html
  Wildflowers

www.auburn.edu/~deancar/
  Wildflowers of Alabama

sac.uky.edu/~mthom0/flora.htm
  Wildflowers of Western Kentucky (links)

www.mmcinc.com/wildflowers/
  The Woodlands Wildflowers

Subject Disciplines:

Art
Science
Social Studies

GENERAL REFERENCE SOURCES

www.icon.org/vlmp/lists.html
  Best of the Web

www.bigbook.com
  Big Book

the-tech.mit.edu/Shakespeare/
  Complete Works of Shakespeare

usinfo.state.gov/usis.html
  Department of State – International
  Information Programs

www.dictionary.com
  Dictionary.com

www.edmunds.com
  Edmunds.com

www.educationindex.com
  Education Index

www.eduhound.com
  EduHound.com

www.pantheon.org/mythica/
  Encyclopedia Mythica

www.fedworld.gov
  FedWorld Information Network Home Page

www.firstgov.com
  FirstGov

www.fedworld.gov/supcourt/index.htm
  FLITE – Supreme Court Decisions

www.irs.gov/forms_pubs/index.html
  Forms and Publications – IRS

(continued)

WEB SITES TO INVESTIGATE DURING THE RESEARCH PROCESS

(continued)

www.einet.net/galaxy.html
  Galaxy

www.123greetings.com
  Greeting Cards

www.go.grolier.com
  Go.grolier.com

iwin.nws.noaa.gov/iwin/main.html
  Interactive Weather Information Network

www.ipl.org
  Internet Public Library

www.julliard.edu
  The Julliard School Gateway
  Library and Archives: Internet Resources

www.libraryspot.com
  LibrarySpot

www.mapquest.com
  Map Quest

www.money.com
  Money.com

www.nasa.gov
  NASA Homepage

www.nationalgeographic.com
  NATIONALGEOGRAPHIC.COM

www.greatwomen.org
  The National Women's Hall of Fame

www.nyse.com
  NYSE
  (New York Stock Exchange)

www.newsweek.com
  Newsweek Front Page

www.familyeducation.com/home
  Parenting advice . . .

www.prairienet.org/pg
  Project Gutenberg Mirror Site

www.researchpaper.com
  Researchpaper.com

www.si.edu
  Smithsonian Institution

www.census.gov/prod/www/statistical-abstract-us.html
  Statistical Abstract of the United States

thomas.loc.gov
  Thomas—US Congress on the Internet

www.aoc.gov
  The United States Capitol

www.usatoday.com
  USA TODAY

lcweb.loc.gov/copyright
  U.S. Copyright Office Home Page

www.washingtonpost.com
  Washington Post.com

www.almanac.com
  Welcome to Almanac.com

www.carnegiehall.org
  WELCOME TO CARNEGIE HALL

fotw.digibel.be/flags
  Welcome to Flags of the World

www.odci.gov/cia/publications/pubs.html
  World Fact Book

www.flags.net
  World Flag Database

Great Research Projects Step by Step

WORKS CITED*

About Infotrac. Gale Company. 3 July 99. <http://www.libraryianet.com>.

About Search. About.com. 23 Sept. 00. <http://www.about.com>.

Academic Abstracts. CD-ROM. Ebsco. 1999.

Advanced Search Help. Altavista. 23 Sept. 00. <http://www.altavista.com>.

Advanced Searching. Lycos. 23 Sept. 00. <http://www.lycos.com>.

Advanced Searching. Webcrawler. 23 Sept. 00. <http://www.webcrawler.com>.

American Business Disc. CD-ROM. InfoUSA. 1999.

Basic Searching. Metacrawler. 23 Sept. 00. <http://www.metacrawler.com>.

"Broadband EduNet." *T.H.E. Journal.* Sept. 2000: 48–50.

Dyrli, Odvard Egil. "Curriculum Hot Spots on the Web 2000." *Curriculum Administrator* Sept. 1999: 67–73.

Ebscohost. 23 Sept. 00. <http://www.slcl.lib.mo.us>.

First Search. 27 December 1999. <http://www.firstsearch.oclc.org>.

General Information about the Westplex Information Network. Westplex Information Network. 26 December 1999. <www.win.org>.

General Search Tips. Excite. 23 Sept. 00. <http://www.excite.com>.

Gibaldi, Joseph. *MLA Style Manual And Guide To Scholarly Publishing.* New York: The Modern Language Association of America. 1998.

Help. Chubba. 23 Sept. 00. <http://www.chubba.com>.

Help. Dogpile. 23 Sept. 00. <http://www.dogpile.com>.

Help. FastSearch. 23 Sept. 00. <http://www.alltheweb.com>.

Help. ProFusion. 23 Sept. 00. <http://www.profusion.com>.

Help. Starting Point. 23 Sept. 00. <http://www.stpt.com>.

Help on Searching. Galaxy. 23 Sept. 00. <http://www.galaxy.com>.

Internet FAQ Archives. FAQS. 30 June 1999. <http://www.faqs/usenet>.

Internet Relay Chat. Westplex Information Network. 30 June 1999. <http://www.win.org/irc.rules.htm>.

Krol, Ed. *The Whole Internet User's Guide and Catalog.* Sebastopol, CA: O'Reilly & Associates, 1994.

New York Times. CD-ROM. Proquest. 1999.

WORKS CITED* *(continued)*

Power Search. Go.com. 23 Sept. 00. <http://www.go.com>.

Search Help. Ixquick. 23 Sept. 00. <http://www.ixquick.com>.

Search Tips. Hotbot. 23 Sept. 00. <http://www.hotbot.com>.

Search Tips. NBCi. 23 Sept. 00. <http://www.nbci.com>.

Search Tips. Yahoo. 23 Sept. 00. <http://www.yahoo.com>.

SIRS. CD-ROM. Sirs Inc. 1999.

Tip. Direct Hit. 23 Sept. 00. <http://www.directhit.com>.

Tips. Northern Light. 23 Sept. 00. <http://www.northernlight.com>.

What Is Usenet?. FAQS. 26 Dec. 1999. <http://www.faqs.org./usenet>.

* This MLA documentation style corresponds with the documentation examples cited on page 36.

Answer Key

SECTION 2 (PAGES 43–67)

2A 1. 500–599 2. 200–299 3. 900–999 4. 600–699 5. 800–899 6. 900–999 7. 300–399; 8. 500–599 9. 700–799 10. 700–799 11. 900–999 12. 600–699 13. 600–699 14. 300–399 15. 600–699 16. 900–999 17. 700–799 18. 700–799 19. 100–199 20. 600–699

2B 1. S 2. T 3. A 4. S 5. T 6. A 7. A, S 8. A 9. S 10. T 11. T 12. S 13. A 14. T 15. T

2C 1. AU/ 2. TI/ 3. SU/ 4. AU/ 5. TI/ 6. SU/ 7. TI/ 8. SU/ 9. SU/ 10. SU/ 11. AU/ 12. TI/ 13. SU/ 14. TI/ 15. AU/ or TI/ 16. AU/ 17. AU/ 18. SU/ 19. AU/ or TI/

2D 1. su/Barbie doll 2. su/cheetah 3. su/barometer 4. su/solar eclipse 5. su/telephone 6. su/moon landing 7. su/light speed 8. su/planets 9. su/alphabet 10. su/stars 11. su/primary colors 12. su/Australian residents 13. su/baseball team 14. su/Himalaya Mountains or Himalayas 15. su/French temperature 16. su/fire prevention 17. su/electricity 18. su/winter solstice 19. su/Newbery Medal 20. su/Hale-Bopp comet or Hale-Bopp

2E 1. su/inhabitants AND Madagascar Islands 2. su/Arabian oryx OR scimitar–horned oryx 3. su/size AND whales NOT blue whale, su/size AND whale family NOT blue whale 4. su/Jupiter AND atmosphere 5. su/crocodiles OR alligators 6. su/rose varieties NOT pink rose, rose AND varieties NOT pink rose 7. su/climate zone AND hot, su/hottest climate zone 8. su/sport injuries NOT football 9. su/soccer OR ice hockey 10. su/hurricane AND fatalities

Note: The keywords within the Boolean commands can be written in any order as long as the correct Boolean operator is listed. For example, **oranges OR apples** can be written **apples OR oranges.**

2F 1. atlas 2. almanac 3. biographical dictionary, encyclopedia 4. encyclopedia 5. almanac, encyclopedia 6. atlas 7. atlas, geographical dictionary 8. almanac, biographical dictionary, encyclopedia 9. almanac 10. biographical dictionary, encyclopedia 11. atlas 12. almanac 13. almanac 14. encyclopedia 15. almanac, encyclopedia, atlas

2G 1. Bartlett's Famous Quotations 2. Reader's Guide 3. Nat'l Geographic Index 4. Brewer's Dictionary of Phrase and Fable 5. Nat'l Geographic Index 6. Nat'l Geographic Index 7. Bartlett's Famous Quotations 8. Reader's Guide 9. Thesaurus 10. Bartlett's Famous Quotations 11. Reader's Guide, Nat'l Geographic Index 12. Reader's Guide 13. Brewer's Dictionary of Phrase and Fable

2H 1. Masterplots 2. Contemporary Authors 3. Magill's Literary Annual 4. Guinness Book of Records 5. Famous First Facts 6. Masterplots 7. Masterplots 8. Masterplots 9. Short Story Index 10. Masterplots 11. Contemporary Authors 12. Magill's Literary Annual 13. Short Story Index

Note: Magill's Literary Annual evaluates books published during the current year. Past volumes can be considered, if the literary work was outstanding.

2I 1. Europa 2. Facts on File 3. Current Biography 4. Yearbook of the United Nations 5. Facts on File, Yearbook of the United Nations 6. Europa 7. Facts on File 8. Europa 9. Yearbook of the United Nations 10. Facts on File 11. Facts on File 12. Facts on File, Europa 13. Facts on File 14. Europa 15. Facts on File

2J 1. Official Congressional Directory 2. Statistical Abstract of the United States 3. Statistical Abstract of the World 4. N.A.D.A. 5. Consumer Reports Buying Guide 6. Official Congressional Directory 7. Statistical Abstract of the United States

8. Official Congressional Directory
9. Congressional Quarterly Almanac
10. Consumer Reports Buying Guide
11. Statistical Abstract of the World

2K 1. G   2. J   3. C   4. N   5. F   6. H   7. M;
8. D   9. K   10. Q   11. A   12. L   13. E
14. I   15. S   16. B   17. P   18. T   19. O
20. R

SECTION 3 (PAGES 69–78)

3A 1. exports AND Irish; exports AND Ireland
2. tornado damage AND Kissimmee AND
Florida   3. military buildup AND Persian Gulf
4. resolution AND United Auto Workers
5. effect AND cigarette smoking AND teenagers   6. effects AND El Nino AND 1997–1998
AND Californian coast   7. nuclear status AND
Pakistan OR nuclear status AND India
8. skating performance AND Tara Lipinski OR
skating performance AND Michelle Kwan

3B 1. black hole AND 1990s   2. sunken ships
AND twentieth century   3. total casualties
AND US wars NOT Vietnamese War   4. warm-
ing effect AND El Nino AND northern
hemisphere   5. toxic agents AND atmosphere
AND health problems   6. changes AND brain
tissue AND Alzheimer's disease   7. clothes
AND 1940s OR clothes AND 1960s NOT shoes

3C 1. InfoTrac   2. InfoTrac   3. EBSCOhost
4. InfoTrac   5. First Search   6. InfoTrac
7. EBSCOhost   8. EBSCOhost   9. First
Search, InfoTrac   10. InfoTrac   11. InfoTrac
12. InfoTrac   13. InfoTrac   14. InfoTrac
15. EBSCOhost   16. InfoTrac   17. InfoTrac
18. First Search

3D 1. SIRS   2. American Business Disc   3. SIRS
4. NY Times, SIRS   5. Academic Abstracts
6. SIRS   7. Academic Abstracts   8. SIRS
9. NY Times   10. SIRS   11. American Business Disc   12. NY Times   13. NY Times
14. SIRS   15. SIRS   16. SIRS   17. Academic
Abstracts

3E 1. 7   2. 4   3. 1, 2   4. 7   5. 3, 6   6. 5   7. 1
8. 1, 2   9. 2   10. 3   11. 4   12. 4

SECTION 4 (PAGES 79–97)

4A 1. answers will vary   2. answers will vary
3. www. Virtual Library and Librarian's Index
4. (+), (–) before quotation marks; quotation

marks around phrases and proper names
5. to designate words appearing as a unit or
to specify words to be included or excluded
within the document   6. hierarchial directory
that promotes sub-searching   7. Answers will
vary.   8. They search many search engines
simultaneously   9. Answers will vary.
10. "California redwoods" +Northwest;
+California +redwoods +Northwest

4B A.   1. damage, 1993 floods   2. rare, white,
Siberian tiger   3. persons, Mt. Everest
4. atmosphere, Jupiter   5. life, Mars   6. St.-
John's-wort, depression   7. garlic, beneficial,
body   8. football, origin, Europe\

B. (answers may vary)   1. disaster
2. unusual   3. climbers   4. air   5. viability
6. despondency   7. useful   8. beginning

4C (answers may vary) A.   1. presidential
2. appointment   3. computer   4. managerial
5. automation   6. mistaken   7. educational
8. political   9. information   10. electrical

B.   television ad, television advertisement,
television advertiser, television advertising,
television addict, television addiction

4D 1. "Mother's Day"   2. "salt-and-pepper" +hair
–red   3. +activated "air bag"   4. "animal activists"; +animal +activists   5. +Cardinal +baseball
+statistics –football   6. "World Cup" +statistics
–dishes   7. "French recipes"   8. "Christmas
tree" –artificial; +Christmas +tree –artificial
9. +disabled +American +veteran; "American
veteran" +disabled   10. "Civil War" +battles;
"Civil War battles"   11. +chromosomal
+abnormalities   12. "April Fools Day"
13. +young +drivers –adult   14. +unfinished
+furniture

4E 1. "Happy Birthday"   2. "miniature golf"
+course; +miniature +golf +course   3. +rising
+crime +rate   4. "Three Musketeers" –candy
5. +windows –glass   6. "Pulitzer Prize winner";
"Pulitzer Prize" +winner   7. "Ronald Reagan"
8. "All Star Game"   9. "Hall of Fame" –football
10. +Apollo –god   11. +Hershey +Pennsylvania
–candy 12. "higher education"   13. "red,
white, and blue"   14. "Lake Michigan"

Note: AND is used if all terms are to be
included within one document. OR can be
used if alternatives are implied or if inclusion
of all terms seems unlikely. As a rule, try AND
first and then OR.

4F 1. sports equipment AND (football OR baseball NOT basketball)   2. (roast beef OR ham OR steak) AND entrees AND (chocolate cake OR apple pie)   3. (Coke OR iced tea OR milk) AND (hamburgers OR hot dogs OR bratwurst)   4. Native American culture AND (Cherokee AND Sioux AND Seneca NOT Mohawk)   5. hitting record AND (Babe Ruth OR Ty Cobb OR Willie Mays)   6. Persian Gulf War casualties NOT reserve units   7. (temperature AND humidity) AND (Chicago OR Detroit OR St. Louis NOT New York City)   8. (benefits AND eyeglasses) AND (benefits AND soft contacts)

4G 1. "French recipes" NOT "American recipes"   2. "baseball rules" OR "football rules"   3. (leprosy and symptoms) AND "death rate"   4. fashions AND 1980s; +fashions +1980s   5. damage AND "Hurricane Camille" +Mississippi; damage AND "Hurricane Camille" AND Mississippi   6. "Dutch Elm disease" AND "American trees"; "Dutch Elm disease" AND trees AND American   7. "tall buildings AND ("Empire State building OR "John Hancock building" OR "Sears Tower")   8. "American League teams" AND statistics AND ("Detroit Lions" AND "Oakland Athletics" NOT "Cleveland Indians")   9. "futurist cars" AND "2030–2050"

4H 1. www.prospernet.com/; surfing, recreation, automotive   2. www.toolcity.net/; cars, model A   3. www.ucr.edu/; car, transportation museum   4. www.bios.niu.edu/; Orion, constellation list   5. www.aminews.com/; ski, index, Colorado

SECTION 5 (PAGES 99–111)

5A 1. D   2. E   3. B   4. C   5. B   6. C   7. B, D   8. C   9. A   10. B, C   11. B   12. A   13. D   14. C   15. C   16. B

Share Your Bright Ideas with Us!

We want to hear from you! Your valuable comments and suggestions will help us meet your current and future classroom needs.

Your name_____Date_____

School name_____Phone_____

School address_____

Grade level taught_____Subject area(s) taught_____Average class size_____

Where did you purchase this publication?_____

Was your salesperson knowledgeable about this product?   Yes_____   No_____

What monies were used to purchase this product?

____School supplemental budget   ____Federal/state funding   ____Personal

Please "grade" this Walch publication according to the following criteria:

Quality of service you received when purchasing .... A	B	C	D	F
Ease of use.. A	B	C	D	F
Quality of content.. A	B	C	D	F
Page layout .... A	B	C	D	F
Organization of material .... A	B	C	D	F
Suitability for grade level .... A	B	C	D	F
Instructional value... A	B	C	D	F

COMMENTS:_____

_____

What specific supplemental materials would help you meet your current—or future—instructional needs?

_____

Have you used other Walch publications? If so, which ones?_____

May we use your comments in upcoming communications?   ____Yes   ____No

Please **FAX** this completed form to **207-772-3105**, or mail it to:

Product Development, J. Weston Walch, Publisher, P.O. Box 658, Portland, ME 04104-0658

We will send you a **FREE GIFT** as our way of thanking you for your feedback. **THANK YOU!**